T0116499

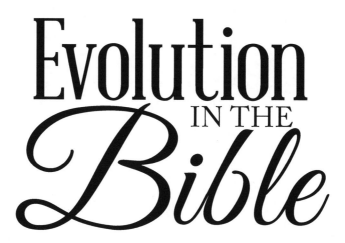

Evolution IN THE Bible

An Integral Overview of the Hebrew Scriptures

Patricia J. Veenema, MDiv.

BALBOA.PRESS
A DIVISION OF HAY HOUSE

Balboa Press books may be ordered through booksellers or by contacting:

Balboa Press
A Division of Hay House
1663 Liberty Drive
Bloomington, IN 47403
www.balboapress.com
844-682-1282

Because of the dynamic nature of the Internet, any web addresses or links contained in this book may have changed since publication and may no longer be valid. The views expressed in this work are solely those of the author and do not necessarily reflect the views of the publisher, and the publisher hereby disclaims any responsibility for them.

The author of this book does not dispense medical advice or prescribe the use of any technique as a form of treatment for physical, emotional, or medical problems without the advice of a physician, either directly or indirectly. The intent of the author is only to offer information of a general nature to help you in your quest for emotional and spiritual well-being. In the event you use any of the information in this book for yourself, which is your constitutional right, the author and the publisher assume no responsibility for your actions.

Any people depicted in stock imagery provided by Getty Images are models, and such images are being used for illustrative purposes only. Certain stock imagery © Getty Images.

All scripture quotations unless otherwise indicated are taken from the NRSV (New Revised Standard Version of the Bible), Copyright © 1989, by the Division of Christian Education of the National Council of the Churches of Christ in the United States of America. Used by permission. All rights reserved. Website

Print information available on the last page.

ISBN: 979-8-7652-3756-4 (sc)
ISBN: 979-8-7652-3757-1 (e)

Library of Congress Control Number: 2022923274

Balboa Press rev. date: 12/30/2022

Dedicated to
EJ Niles

In Memory of
Harv Morrow
And
Don Beck

Foreword

I am pleased to be invited to present a foreword to this book. While being in no way a biblical scholar I recognize the importance of Pat's primary question. Beliefs are at the root of so many of the world's disputes and there are so many contexts in which the bible is invoked as an authority in support of widely different viewpoints.

My own expertise is in the model developed by Clare W. Graves and subsequently called Spiral Dynamics (SD). The model itself is wide in perspective, comprehensive in its coverage of human thought and behavior. It describes why we think in the ways we do. It presents those different humans views of our world and our priorities for how to live in it as an adaptive process. Our thinking systems change to respond to the demands of our life conditions in a way which resembles the genetics of biological adaptation to varying ecosystem contexts. It is a psycho-social Darwinism.

In order to provide a perspective on views of the bible it is necessary to take a slice through the richness, let go of the reasons and simplify SD to a core set of outcomes. As an enthusiast for the wider model, I encourage readers to discover what lies behind the stages of thinking that it describes. An introductory overview of the wider theory can be found in this book's Appendix. Nevertheless, this simplification has a great deal to offer to any student of human thought and therefore to anyone exploring the relationship between their own thinking and the stories and teachings of the Bible. This book explores that offering.

My own way of looking at the sequence of worldviews is to note that it sets something alongside the notion that God created all that we see and are and that "He" created us in his image. In contrast, our views of God or the Divine are reflections and projections of how we see the world, and how we see ourselves. In that sense we create God in our image. These reflections and projections are opened up in this book for us to see more clearly the way in which the Bible itself emerged over time, had its own development and was written by a variety of hands. Beyond that it offers a way to see the further development of thought since it was written and explore the ways in which more recent worldviews affect our interpretations of its content.

Pat's book is a study guide, and the virtue of this presentation is that it doesn't tell us what to think. Instead, it presents us with a lot of questions that we can ask of ourselves, regarding the bible itself and about its writers. It makes many of those questions explicit and provides guidance for the journey. It is an invitation to explore the territory of thought, and of Judeo-Christian religious thought in particular. What are you seeing, and how are you looking? It is a rich opportunity for expansion, and I hope that readers will enjoy and benefit from that.

Jon Freeman
Trainer of Spiral Dynamics at ValueMatch. Director of Future Considerations, Author of: The Science of Possibility.
September 2022

Acknowledgments

The original idea to overlay the Documentary Hypothesis with Spiral Dynamics came out the work of Rev. EJ Niles, who taught this evolutionary lens to many Unity students from her pulpit and from the classroom lectern. In Seminary, as I unpacked my embedded theology and re-formed my understanding of the Bible, EJ's pastoral responses to my sometimes-emotional reactions provided courage and sanity to continue the excavation. I appreciate her late husband Harv Morrow for providing "Harv Slides." (complex PowerPoint slides that illustrate the authorship of the Bible over the centuries.) EJ told Don Beck of her work, who heartily encouraged her to publish it. I am grateful that EJ and her ministry Spiral Pathways supported me as I wrote.

I acknowledge that Unity Institute and Seminary provided a safe space for me to transform my understanding of God and the Bible. I acknowledge the teachers of my childhood: my parents, ministers, Sunday School teachers, and Bible teachers for giving me a thorough Biblical education. Without that rich Bible foundation, I would not have been able to write this book.

I'm grateful to Richard Elliott Friedman whose books were constantly at my side as I wrote. I am also grateful to Marcus Borg, Israel Finkelstein, Garry Stevens, and Epimetheus.

My thanks to Doris Rikkers and Ellen Hamersma who edited and advised. I appreciate Darla Henry, Cindy White, Barbara Keller, Cheryl Driscoll, Lou Therrell, study groups from Unity of Olympia and Unity of Tustin, and countless students who suggested, encouraged, and discussed the manuscript in our online classes. And to those who supported me financially in publishing this manuscript, it is an honor to know people from many areas of my life stepped forward to help get this information to readers.

I launch the book knowing my research will never be concluded, and excited to anticipate responses from you, my readers.

Contents

"In his evolution man has apparently always moved in
cycles; but each time he comes again to his starting place
he seems to be a little in advance of his former state." [1]
~ Charles Fillmore. *Mysteries of Genesis*

"He who studies Mind may know how to "discern the signs
of the times." He becomes familiar with certain underlying
principles, and he recognizes them in their different masks in
"the whirligig of time." Under the veil of historical symbology
the Scriptures portray the movements of Mind in its different
cycles of progress. These cycles repeat themselves over and over
again, but each time on a higher plane. Thus the sphere or
circle is a type of the complete Mind, but in manifestation the
circles are piled one on top of another in an infinite spiral." [2]
~ Charles Fillmore *Talks on Truth*

Introduction

It has been the bestselling book since the invention of the printing press. It has influenced religion, culture, government, economics, and ethics. It has had more influence on Western civilization than any other book and has been the bedrock of western culture for over 3000 years.

The Bible provides comfort, inspiration, and guidance, and is often misinterpreted, causing social, spiritual, and psychological pain, and countless ethical dilemmas and debates. It has been misunderstood, misquoted, and presents a God many are ashamed to align themselves with. Many Christians and Jews no longer read the Bible. It sits on the shelf collecting dust while they try to make sense of their religion within the context of modern worldviews.

I grew up with the Bible as the inspired, infallible Word of God for All Ages. I believed that there was no other legitimate sacred text. I accepted the Heidelberg Catechism (1563) as true because every statement of faith is footnoted with a reference to a Bible verse. Tangled in the web of trusting my elders and Calvinist teachings, I abandoned logic to affirm my faith. In my twenties, I became an academic and professional thinker, and my faith could not rise to that level of reasoning. I put the Bible on the shelf and channeled my focus into conscientious Christian social action. Thirty years later, when I responded to the intuitive call to the ministry, I was required to open the Bible again and begin my reconciliation with it. I studied Modern and Post-Modern Christian and atheist scholars: John Shelby Spong, Richard Elliott Friedman, Bart Erdmann, Marcus Borg, John

Dominic Crosson, and others from the Jesus Seminar. I struggled, argued, and cried over the pain and confusion the Bible had imprinted into my psyche, and eventually came out of the Unity Institute and Seminary with a healthy, though completely transformed, way of relating to that ancient sacred text.

This is a book for the layperson to learn what is rarely discussed outside of seminary. The truth is, when discussed in seminary it is typically ignored and denied. Ministers don't know what to do with this information and they ignore it because it shakes their traditional faith foundations. The raw truth about it can catapult a person into a major faith crisis, but as our world becomes less and less familiar with the Bible, it is valuable for us to return to it to see where we've come from and how it influences our culture even now in the 21st century. I wrote this book to provide tools so that the reader can reconcile with the ancient teachings and put them into perspective based on the values of today's world.

As you read this book, my hope is that you will come to a place of clarity, appreciation, and liberation concerning the Hebrew Scriptures. Like transparencies on an overhead projector, we will overlay two scholarly models or tools: the Documentary Hypothesis and Spiral Dynamics. We will be able to discern the evolving cultural perspectives about the Divine.

You're on your way to finding spiritual peace and freedom to perceive the Bible as an evolutionary tool. The spiritual seeker of the 21st century knows they don't need sacred writing to find God. Humans never did.

Chapter 1

Which God of the Bible?

S ince the beginning of our awareness, humans have intuitively sensed that an invisible Power and Presence is the First Cause of all things. The Bible's very first verse begins with that assumption. "In the beginning, when God created the heavens and the earth…" (Genesis 1:1, P writer). "In the day that Yahweh (YHWH) created the earth and the heavens…" (Genesis 2:1, J writer).

Acknowledgment of this invisible Presence and Power provides meaning to our lives. It offers a sense of belonging and security, and it offers us a reason to accept "what is." God is an Absolute to most of us, but our understanding of "God" continually evolves. As we grow our awareness of our world and our place in it, we gradually and profoundly adjust our understanding of "God." And, vice versa: as we clarify our understanding of the divine, we clarify our understanding of ourselves.

Before humankind developed logic and reasoning, we attributed things we didn't understand to this mystical entity. We engaged our creative imagination and intuition to visualize this power and presence, the great mystery of our spiritual source. As we developed through the levels described by Spiral Dynamics our intellect matured, and our worldview expanded and became more complex. So did our perception of God.

Our perception of God is affected by our culture and the era in which we live. Most of the time, in multiple cultures, "this God," by whatever name and whatever image, is the only God that is legitimate. We will argue, fight, and even die over these beliefs about this mysterious Power and Presence.

Which God of the Bible do people believe in? Do you believe in the one that champions magic? Or is it the one that wins your wars? Maybe it's the God who loves justice? Or perhaps you can only accept a God that is Principle and Mind. Whichever one it is, do you tend to insist that you have the right idea of God, and everyone else is misled?

In the 1890s, at the onset of the Unity movement, Dr. H. Emilie Cady wrote a series of articles for Charles and Myrtle Fillmore who published the Modern Thought Magazine. This series was subsequently published as a book titled "Lessons In Truth," and it became Unity School of Practical Christianity's primary textbook.

In her lesson "Unity of the Spirit," Cady attempts to explain how people have different perceptions of what she calls "the stupendous whole." She invites her readers to imagine that a dozen people are standing on one side of a wall that has openings of various sizes. Each person looks through a hole to see what's on the other side. Their view will necessarily be limited by the size of the opening. Cady writes, "each sees all there is within a certain radius. He says, 'I see the whole world; in it are trees and fields.' Another, through a larger opening, has a more extended view; he says: 'I see trees and fields and houses; I see the whole world.' The next one, looking through a still larger opening, exclaims: 'Oh! You are all wrong! I alone see the whole world; I see trees and fields and houses and rivers and animals!'"[3]

We will observe in this study that each stage of the evolutionary model has a wider aperture with which to see the world. Those whose worldviews are limited by egoic blinders are poised to argue that "they alone can see the whole world." They cite religious texts and dogma to defend their stance, unaware that those religious ideas arose from ancient worldviews that are very limited in scope.

Which God of the Bible?

What do people know and not know about the God of the Bible? In a 2018 survey, about half of the U.S. population said they believed in the God that is in the Bible.[4] Perhaps, then, a more applicable question is: Which God of the Bible do people believe in? In the survey, people describe this God as a powerful, knowing, benevolent, and active deity who loves all people regardless of their faults and protects them. This perception of God is supported by carefully selected passages from the Bible and ignores the passages that describe God as fickle, narcissistic, and jealous. We read the Bible selectively and with different lenses and blinders depending on what we want to believe or learn.

Many modern thinkers have consciously or subconsciously rejected the Bible. But no matter how much we resist or ignore it, not one of us can completely ban it from affecting us. The Bible's influence is at the foundation of Western civilization. It has shaped centuries of public policy, church governance, ethics, race and gender issues, literature, movies, music, customs, and taboos. Even as the U.S. population is increasingly less religious, this book continues to inform the collective conscious in subtle and profound ways.

The Hebrew Bible or what Christians call the "Old Testament" provides insights into the roots of the monotheistic trio of religions: Judaism, Christianity, and Islam, and offers numerous examples of the way humankind has evolved their understanding of God. Throughout this book, the word "Bible" refers to the Hebrew Bible.

In this study, we will observe that the collected writings of the Bible chronicle a dynamically evolving understanding of the divine, illustrating that humankind's perception of the divine keeps changing and expanding. This is not to say that "God" has changed. How we perceive the divine naturally evolves as we move through our developmental stages. Our perception of God is in direct correlation with our perception and understanding of our world.

A Variety of Lenses

How we approach the Bible affects how we understand it. At different times and stages of our lives, we use different lenses to read the scriptures. When reading this time-honored collection of writings, each of us will apply any combination of lenses: literal, devotional, metaphysical, historical, and evolutionary.

In 2001, Marcus Borg declared that the "conflict about how to see and read the Bible is the single greatest issue dividing Christians in North America today."[5] Indeed, it is cited during debates about ecology, evolution, race relations, justice, economics, morals, abortion, migration, diet, education, sexuality, marriage, family structures, and even tattoos. Through the course of history, passionate arguments about these scriptures have occupied many synagogues, churches, seminaries, universities, coffee shops, and dinner tables. Many individuals have been judged, shunned, and emotionally wounded by a literal interpretation of the Bible's messages. Many modern thinkers who grew up with the Bible enter adulthood no longer able to turn to the Bible as a spiritual guide. They have incorporated science, psychology, and reason into their perception of the divine and found that the Bible does not present their idea of a loving God. They see a vengeful God in the Hebrew Scriptures and a loving God in the Christian scriptures and conclude that the Jews and the Christians must have different Gods, or that perhaps God Itself has evolved. It is not that "God" evolved, it's that our perception of this Mystery has evolved as we evolved our worldview.

- The Literal Lens. Children use a "literal" lens, learning each Bible story as if it was fact, admiring brave heroes and prophets, kings and servants who were devoted to God. Adults using a literal lens view the words of the Bible as the "downloaded" or channeled words of God, and consider the laws, events, characters, and miracles as divinely true and valid; the immutable, inspired, and infallible "Word of God." People who use this approach might say, "The Bible says…," to cite specific verses to further or oppose a cause they feel strongly about.

- The Devotional Lens. Some consider the Bible as a sacred devotional tool. They faithfully read through the liturgical readings, endeavoring to discover hidden truths to build their faith. Some have a rather magical belief about the Bible: you can open it anywhere, and the reading will have a personal message from God. More than one lens can be applied at one time. For example, devoutly religious people often use both the literal lens and the devotional lens.

- The Metaphysical Lens. This lens includes a wide variety of approaches including maieutic, metaphorical, and metaphysical interpretation, and takes into consideration the styles of literature—mythology, allegory, and parable. Some individuals read the Bible as any great piece of literature, seeking to unlock the hidden meaning. They might use concordances, parallel translations, and a Metaphysical Bible Dictionary to help them understand the meaning and apply it to their personal spiritual growth and awakening.

- The Historical Lens. To make rational sense of the time-honored texts, some people seek extra-biblical proof to ascertain historical veracity. They research the findings of archeologists, linguists, anthropologists, and historians. Some who read the Bible through the historical lens dismiss it for its inaccuracies and contradictions, unable to value it for its devotional appeal. Some are appalled by the negative images of God portrayed there, and vehemently reject it because it appears to be "written solely by humans in an ignorant, superstitious, and cruel age, from an unenlightened era."[6]

- The Evolutionary Lens. This book suggests a new way of being Biblically literate. It invites you to temporarily set aside any previous approach to the Bible and read the stories and lessons in an entirely new way by using an evolutionary perspective or lens. Through this approach, you may release the Bible as sacred, but you may discover it to be an integral tool on your spiritual journey.

Using a model of the evolution of consciousness, we can read the Bible as a document that displays how we as a human species have evolved our thinking and our understanding of God. The evolutionary approach to reading the Bible can help us reconcile with the religion of our childhood, mature our spiritual understanding, and address the questions emerging with twenty-first-century spirituality. With an evolutionary approach, we de-mystify the Bible and are free to study it without the bias of culturally imposed religious dogma, interpretations, translations, and concordances. We come to see that we are not obligated to give these writings the same significance as our great-grandparents gave them, and we develop respect for those who perceive God and the Bible differently than we do. We encounter opportunities to reconcile with those stories and rules of conduct that are inappropriate, abhorrent, and shameful to our Modern/Post-Modern[7] consciousness. We grow into greater compassion toward "the other," including our ancestors, and we get a chance to mature spiritually and emotionally. The evolutionary lens helps the individual release fear and resistance about the Bible and opens the door to recognize shadow thoughts and feelings, heal wounds, and identify conditioned thinking and unquestioned beliefs.

The evolutionary approach is an essential tool to help us integrate or at least tolerate all the other lenses holistically. The evolutionary lens invites us to practice an integral view, honoring each lens as useful and valid for the individual and the collective, as we assimilate all facets and stages into a holistic understanding of the divine. This approach does not replace it, rather it compliments other methods of Bible interpretation.

Why propose a new way to view the Bible?

Conventional instruction about the Bible is outdated and misinformed, based on theories of authorship that do not consider the past two hundred years of Biblical scholarship. With the application of two key tools, Spiral Dynamics, and the Documentary Hypothesis, along with insights from archeology, we can see a remarkable evolutionary treasure contained within the Bible. In this study, we will see that the Bible provides indicators that map the evolution of humankind's perception of God, and it provides a priceless illustration that the evolution of consciousness is continuously in process. And because the evolution of the collective consciousness illustrated in the Bible parallels the evolution of individual consciousness, we can use it to understand the personal evolving perception of God and humankind. This approach informs us about the value systems from which we've come, and the stage of faith we find ourselves in now. For a twenty-first-century spiritual seeker, using an evolutionary lens is potentially the most meaningful reason for revisiting these ancient scriptures.

Seeing the Bible with a new lens can cause much cognitive dissonance but it can also produce a sense of freedom. This approach can clear up misunderstandings about the Bible, open a door toward healing wounds caused by childhood Bible instruction, and offer insights into the patterns and trends of worldviews not only in ancient times but also in today's spiritual evolution. The evolutionary lens provides an avenue to address confusion and misunderstanding about Bible writings and to gain insights into the patterns, trends, and trajectories of evolving value systems in individual and collective human development. During this study, you will clarify your understanding of the Bible as scripture, and you will discover it to be an integral treasure to understand the evolution of human awareness of the divine.

The Traditional Divisions of the Hebrew Scriptures

In this study, we will focus only on the Hebrew Bible, because it gives us the long-view perspective necessary to perceive an evolution of thought.

Jewish readers refer to their sacred scripture as the *Tanakh*, an acronym for the three traditional divisions of the Hebrew Bible: The Torah, the Nevi'im, and the Ketuvim. In English: the Law, the Prophets, and the Writings.

Throughout this book, we will refer to the Tanakh as the "Hebrew Bible." "Bible" comes from the Greek phrase *ta Biblia*, which means "the books," an expression Hellenistic Jews used to describe their sacred books, which were canonized between 200 BCE–200 CE. Jews, Catholics, and Protestants all have different arrangements of the Hebrew Scriptures. Those differences are mostly structural and will not significantly affect the focus of this book.

Traditionally, an overview of the Hebrew Scriptures would follow the traditional structure of the Tanakh: The Torah, The Nevi'im, and the Ketuvim.

The Torah: The first five books of the Hebrew Bible are also known as "the books of Moses." These books contain narratives and instructions or "law." They are the foundation of the Jewish identity and have traditionally assumed Moses' authorship. Christians call these first five books "the Pentateuch." The narrative is written (roughly) between 1000 BCE and 500 BCE.

The Nevi'im: The writings of the prophets that are traditionally divided into The Former Prophets and the Latter Prophets, spanning about 500 years. Some of these writings are full of compassion, others are filled with condemnation.

The Ketuvim: The "Writings" or "Wisdom Writings" are a collection of sacred poems, hymns, philosophical discourses, love poems, apocalyptic literature, and short fiction stories, mostly written in the later years, but some, like the Psalms, are a collection of poems that represent about 1000 years of Hebrew literature.

The traditional divisions do not consider when the books were written, so it is not helpful to an evolutionary approach. The accepted ordering of the writings in the Hebrew Bible is not in any kind of chronological order neither regarding when they were written nor in the order of when the events occurred. For example, inserted into writings from the ninth century BCE are passages from five hundred years later.

Since the mid-1800s when "The Documentary Hypothesis" was published, most scholars have followed the thesis that the account of events, the names, places, poems, songs, and plots were written by different people from very different eras, then spliced together as if from one storyteller by an anonymous editor who decided what to add and what to delete. When you view the Table of Contents of the Bible, do not assume that the books are organized by the dates of the events. Do not assume they are organized by when they were written. We will apply the Documentary Hypothesis and other biblical scholarship to know when the books were written. The evolutionary lens structures the study on "who wrote it and when" to see the writers' worldview (and God-view) at the time of writing.

The writers of these ancient texts were, of course, influenced by the dominant consciousness of their time. Their stories of the people and the laws and customs provide an excellent source from which we can discern human consciousness at the times of the writings. We will overlay the critically acclaimed Spiral Dynamics Integral model and apply what we know about the writers' emergent historical, political, economic, cultural, and collective consciousness to give us an understanding of their perception of themselves and their God. The Spiral Dynamics integral model shines a spotlight on the Hebrew Bible's unique gift to humanity: it portrays how we have evolved our understanding of the divine and our spiritual identity. We come to see that the Bible doesn't define "God." Rather the Bible describes the human perception of "God" at different stages in our evolutionary journey. God has not changed. Humankind has evolved its understanding of God.

Evolutionary Lens Informs the Traditional Divisions

In this study, we will observe that humanity has evolved its understanding of the divine, as told by the ancient writers, the middle writers, and the latter writers. The evolutionary lens is intended to enhance and fully inform us so that our understanding of the Bible is clarified, enriched, and enlightened. By taking an evolutionary approach, we respectfully reorganize the writings based on their date of origin. The writings of the Hebrew Bible arose from three distinct phases which roughly align with the traditional divisions, however, some of the books must be moved from one division to another based on when they were written. When we do that, three worldviews become readily apparent, and we get a clear picture of the evolving consciousness that these writers represent.

Restructuring the writings by date of origin allows us to step through the eras and identify the message, intentions, and worldview of the authors. But restructuring is not as easy as you might think. Scholars have learned that within some of the books, various voices from different centuries are woven intricately together.

The earliest writings in the Bible came out in the 900s BCE. These writings are found in the Torah and the "Deuteronomistic History" (Deuteronomy and Joshua, Judges, Samuel, and Kings), but they are interwoven with writings that were produced hundreds of years later, making it almost impossible to decipher who wrote what and when. In this study, we will learn that four different voices from two distinct eras contributed to the Torah and the Deuteronomistic History.

The next group of writings was produced in the 800-500s BCE. These books include law, mythology, poetry, and theological discourses (prophecies), as well as revisions and additions to the older writings. They were written over three political periods: the divided kingdom period, the period after the fall of Israel, and the period surrounding the fall of Judah.

The final group of writings, mostly the Wisdom Writings, originated after 500 BCE, during the Second Temple Period. They represent a collection of writings from mostly unidentified voices recording personal observations of God and humanity. These writings are stand-alone pieces that reflect the writer's awareness of life and God.

In this book about the Bible, we'll notice how humankind has evolved its understanding of that which we call "God." We will use two key tools to gain this understanding: The Documentary Hypothesis and Spiral Dynamics. Together, these tools will provide us with the authorship and cultural context of the Bible and will resolve many of the questions and misinformation we've had about the Bible.

Mythology and Theology

Mythology is an essential building block of culture. It develops and instructs a people's identity, worldview, values, and faith. Mythology exposes their political and social biases and fears, and their understanding of themselves and their relationship to God. The Bible was assembled from material written by many people with different perspectives influenced by their worldviews, life conditions, and experiences. Some of this work has historical validity, and some parts are mythology.

The idea that the Bible is largely myth can be shocking to one who has read the Bible with a Literal lens: faithfully accepting the Bible's mystical claims without question. The idea that all the stories in the Torah are not factual and are just mythology can shake a person's faith!

Consider that *myth* is not a negative word. Classifying a story as a "myth" declares that the story is lacking in fact and reason, but it is rich with truth and insight into the human consciousness. A myth is true because it is effective, not because it gives us historically proven information. The focus is on the messages enfolded in the stories. Myth, although fiction, conveys the peoples' identity and their worldview, which is extremely helpful to our study of the evolution of consciousness.

Hebrew Myth and Its Heroes

People who did not grow up with the Bible find the stories and characters foreign and the quotes unfamiliar when they are first introduced to this body of literature. To benefit fully from reading this book, you will need to invest some time getting to know the basic Bible stories and the names of the people who are the main characters. If you are unfamiliar with the Bible, you will find suggestions for reading essential stories at the end of the chapter. At the very least, you should know the patriarchs and the heroes of the Hebrew story. We will explore them briefly here.

Pre-History

The earliest writers wrote stories that, if they happened, would have occurred hundreds of years before 1000 BCE. Their accounts convey pre-historical allegories and the laws, rituals, and covenants with Abraham, Isaac, and Jacob (who are referred to as the patriarchs, thus they are from the Patriarchal period). Also included is the heroic character Moses who defies the Pharaoh of Egypt and leads the people out of slavery. This prehistoric mythology chronicles the descendants of the Patriarchs who, armed with the ark of the covenant and with their God, YHWH (Yahweh), complete their forty-year journey of exile and wanderings and settle in Canaan, the "land flowing with milk and honey." (Exodus 3: 8, 17) At the end of Deuteronomy, the final book of the Torah, Moses brings the people to the promised land and YHWH appoints Joshua as successor to Moses.

Biblical archeologists have yet to find evidence to prove any of the events or the existence of any of the characters before the United Monarchy circa 1000 BCE. It is doubtful that Egypt held the Hebrew people as slaves. Egypt was a major power at the time, but although they kept records of trade and transactions, they did not mention anything about Hebrew slaves. Only a small portion of the people may have been held in Egypt.[8] The story of the Exodus might

12

have been developed as a metaphor for the struggle the Hebrews experienced as they tried to establish themselves in the land that had been governed by Egypt before its recession from the area in the 1200s BCE.

Three Patriarchs of the Faith

The pre-historical stories of the patriarchs: Abraham, Isaac, and Jacob remind the Hebrew people of their covenant with God; they were chosen by their God to be his loyal people and they would occupy the land designated for them. In plain language, God's covenant was, "You be faithful to me, and I will give you safety and prosperity." (Genesis 12 and 15) These patriarchs and their wives: Abraham and Sarah, Isaac and Rebecca, and Jacob and his sister-wives Leah and Rachel are more than characters in the stories, they represent kindness, justice, and truth, the spiritual DNA of the Hebrew identity. These three main traits run through the stories and holidays of the Jewish tradition.[9] (There were other wives and other children. For example, the child born of Sarah's Egyptian handmaiden Hagar was Ishmael, who had twelve sons and is the ancestor of Muhammad, the founder of Islam. Genesis 16, 17, 21, and 25).

God promised Abraham prosperity and growth. According to the writer of this story, God said to Abram (later renamed Abraham), "Do not be afraid, Abram, I am your shield; your reward shall be very great. Look toward heaven and number the stars[10] if you are able to count them. So shall your descendants be. I am the Lord who brought you from Ur, to give you this land to possess" (Genesis 15: 1,5,7). Genesis 15: 13-16 inserts a narrative about Abram's dream with prophecies of terror to come, which was inserted into the story hundreds of years later from when it took place. The dream "foretells" the future of the nation. Abraham and his wife Sarah are the patriarch and matriarch of the Jewish people.

God reiterates his promise to Abraham's grandson Jacob and renames him "Israel." The story is told that while Jacob was on his way to reconcile with his brother Esau, an unidentified man showed up from nowhere and wrestled with Jacob all night long. Jacob said he would not let go of the man until he blessed Jacob (Genesis 32). A later writer connects this story with the covenant promise: God said, "Be fruitful and multiply; a nation and a company of nations shall come from you, and kings shall spring from you. The land which I gave to Abraham, and Isaac I will give to you, and I will give the land to your descendants after you." (Genesis 35: 10-11)

Three Heroes of the Faith

Moses, Joshua, and Elijah are perhaps the most highly influential and inspirational leaders of the Hebrew faith. They are archetypes of a Messianic figure, and in Christianity, are considered precursors to Jesus. When Jesus asked his disciples, "Who do people say that I am?" Elijah was one of the names mentioned. (Mark 8: 28) The writer of the gospel of Matthew, whose target audience was the Jews of Jerusalem, refers to two of the three heroes during Jesus' transfiguration. "Suddenly there appeared to them Moses and Elijah, talking with [Jesus]" (Matthew 17: 3).

These "men of God" (Moses, Joshua, and Elijah) have extraordinary access to God's thoughts and God's miraculous powers. They are the mythological heroes of the Hebrew Scriptures. Their existence is not questioned, but their abilities are likely not factual.

Moses: The book of Exodus is filled with the message that Moses is a special man of YHWH. His life is miraculously spared despite a pharaoh's decree that all first-born Hebrew boys be killed. (Exodus 1) He is called to do a mission beyond human possibility. He sees God in unlikely and unique ways. He is considered to have had a personal revelation of God's word. He is "bigger than life" and his tale is so "tall" that people believed for centuries that he alone, through God's inspiration, wrote all five books of the Torah.

Moses was a divinely guided leader of the people. God appeared directly to him as a burning bush, (Exodus 3) to tell him to lead the people of Israel out of slavery in Egypt and into Canaan, the Promised Land (called this because the land was promised to the patriarchs). During this emancipation process, God sent horrible plagues (Exodus 7-11) through Moses that eventually convinced the pharaoh to let the people leave Egypt. Shortly after leaving Egypt, Moses stretched out his hand and parted the waters of the Reed Sea[11]. (Exodus 14) His walking stick was imbued with divine powers so that he could transform water from stagnant into drinkable. (Exodus 18) He was told directly by God how to help the people when they were in distress and was given supernatural signs from heaven: the pillar of fire and smoke, (Exodus 13) and the manna that appeared on the ground each morning. (Exodus 16) He led the people out of bondage in Egypt, through their wilderness experience to the Promised Land. Most of this legend was preserved through a song that the people sang, recorded in Exodus 15.

Moses is described as the law-giver for the wandering people. Exodus 19 tells us that he alone received the Ten Commandments directly from God and brought them to the people. These laws were eventually the ethical basis for the Kingdom of Israel/Judah for generations to come. (But there are two sets of commandments. We will study this further in chapters 5 and 6.)

Joshua: The books of Exodus, Numbers, Deuteronomy, and Joshua cover the life of Joshua. (circa 1300 BCE). The stories tell us that he, like Moses, met YHWH and was told to take off his shoes because the ground upon which he was standing was holy. (compare Exodus 3: 5 and Joshua 5: 15) He was one of the twelve spies who scouted out the land of Canaan. He assumed leadership from Moses and continued to lead the people into Canaan. Joshua's story involves encounters with enemies just as Moses' story does, and YHWH gives Joshua supernatural powers to defeat those enemies. He led the battle against Jericho, (Joshua 6) and YHWH caused the sun and moon to stand still at Joshua's request. (Joshua 10)

Elijah: Elijah's story is set in the ninth century BCE when Israel and Judah were separate nations. He had direct access to divine powers and divine thought. He accurately predicted a drought, miraculously filled a widow's oil jars, and raised her son from death. (1ˢᵗ Kings 17: 22) With the power of his God YHWH, he triumphed over the priests of Baal, killed them all with a sword, and ended the drought he had predicted. He outran King Ahab's horse-drawn chariot (1ˢᵗ Kings 18: 46). At a mountain called Horeb, Elijah had his famous encounter with God as a sound of sheer silence (1ˢᵗ Kings 19: 12) Elijah doesn't die. He is taken up in a whirlwind to heaven in a chariot of fire and horses of fire. (2ⁿᵈ Kings 2: 11).

Processing This Chapter

(the numbers are for reference only and do not indicate a suggested order or importance)

1. Apply: How was the Bible presented to you as a child? Do you still hold these views? How do you see the Hebrew Scriptures now?
2. Respond: It has been said that the Hebrew Bible is "one-third literature, one-third history, and one-third theology."[12] If you were raised with a literal interpretation of the Bible, how does this idea affect your thoughts, feelings, and beliefs about the religion of your childhood?
3. Reflect: Did you have a period when you were involved in a study of the Bible? Did you experience another era in your life when you shelved the book and never looked at it? What was the difference between these times in your life? Did your values and perceptions change the way you treated the Bible?
4. Learn more about the stories: If you are unfamiliar with the characters or the content of the Bible, consider reading a children's Bible to get the gist of the stories. A handy "Who's Who" of the Bible can be found on the website "Practically

Metaphysical." http://practicallymetaphysical.com/index.php/overview-hebrew-scriptures/bible-outline-hebrew-scriptures/

5. Learn more about the Torah: YouTube videos:
   a. Overview of early Judaism Part 1: *The Family of the Patriarchs and Moses.* 8:25 minutes. World History. Khan Academy. Feb 9, 2017, https://youtu.be/cP-fdixB1Zc
   b. Overview of early Judaism Part 2: *From Moses to the End of the Second Temple Period.* 7:44 minutes. World History. Khan Academy. Feb 9, 2017, https://youtu.be/iBWCZxyElIM
   c. Crash Course in Torah Session 1: *The Basic Breakdown.* Avraham Goldhar provides an overall breakdown of the first five books. Peek into the minute divisions of the Torah. 3:40 minutes https://youtu.be/4HJS5uiIxRY
   d. Crash Course in Torah: Session 2: *The Family of Israel: Creation—Tower of Babel.* Avraham Goldhar, 7:15 minutes. https://youtu.be/kRpva5aDNrI
   e. Crash Course in Torah: Session 3: *Patriarchs and Matriarchs of the Jewish People* (part 1). Avraham Goldhar, 4:04 minutes. https://youtu.be/stMsjlztCxY
   f. Crash Course in Torah: Session 4: *Patriarchs and Matriarchs of the Jewish People* (part 2). Avraham Goldhar, 6:52 minutes.

6. Jeopardy Activity: If you're studying this book with a group of people who don't know the characters of the early Israel allegory, create a Jeopardy game. Listed below are some of the notable characters of early Hebrew myth, in order of appearance. Write a short definition for eight of the people listed in the form of a Jeopardy answer (i.e. "He is known as the founding father of the covenant." "Answer: Who is Abraham?") Abraham, Sarah, Isaac, Rebekah, Jacob, Leah, Rachel, Joseph, Moses, Aaron, Joshua, Samuel, Saul, David, Solomon, Elijah.

Chapter 2

Tool #1: Spiral Dynamics

To read the Bible with an Evolutionary lens, we first establish a credible evolutionary model, Spiral Dynamics. The following is a very brief introduction to the Spiral Dynamics model. Included here is the bare minimum of information about the model to apply it to this study of the Hebrew Scriptures. The Appendix at the back of this book, a thorough introduction, will provide details about the Spiral Dynamics model that aren't addressed here.

The Spiral Dynamics model grew from an extensive study to understand the psyche of the healthy mature adult. Dr. Clare Graves, the creator of the model, observed that all humans develop or evolve through predictable developmental stages toward maturity. The adult grows through stages too, and the quest for full maturity is never-ending. Graves observed that society evolves through similar stages through the course of our collective evolution. He created a model that indicates an oscillating pattern of values and priorities, that expands as it matures.

The spiral shape indicates that a worldview begins with a narrow point of focus, then expands with each developmental stage and increases in breadth, diversity, and complexity, while including the values of the developmental stages it has already experienced. For example, the infant has a very small circle of awareness. As the baby grows into the next stages, (toddler, pre-school, school-age, and young adult...) the worldview or circle of belonging expands.

Collective consciousness has done the same over the hundreds of thousands of years of our evolution. The cultural worldview expands into increasingly wider circles of complexity and awareness. (more diversity, more inclusiveness, more chaos, and more demands).

The Spiral Dynamics model is often summarily dismissed by those who are anti-hierarchical. They forget that in the natural world, "hierarchy" is a healthy element of evolution. The human's perception and interaction with their world evolve in a predictable, sequential, developmental pattern. Each stage builds upon the earlier one, so each stage is more complex: from simple social structure to complex societies; from literal thinking to abstract; from childish dependency to autonomous self-determination. Similar to Maslow's Hierarchy of Needs, a healthy early childhood becomes a firm foundation for the success of subsequent stages. One stage is not "better" than another, but each successive stage is more expansive and more effective in affecting change.

In the next few chapters, as we take an evolutionary tour through the Bible, we will consider the concept "Transcend and Include." As human beings grow toward psycho-social-spiritual maturity, we "transcend" (release or leave behind) the limitations of the earlier level and the beliefs that are not valued in the next stage of development. And we "include" (integrate or carry with us) aspects of the earlier structure into the new paradigm. This is a simple idea, and it provides profound insights into mental and societal health.

At the time when one vMeme is no longer effective and the evolutionary urge is strong, a "Transformational Dilemma" begins. In society, new innovative ideas emerge into the collective consciousness. These ideas confront the unhealthy behaviors of the established vMeme. The new worldview is impatient with the old, which resists the changes. The "Transformational Dilemma" can occur on the individual evolutionary journey, too, particularly when the shift is urgent and pressing. When one feels the divine discontent to shift into a different paradigm, life can become dynamic: filled with choices, releases, courageous steps of faith, and sometimes a loss of friends and social belonging.

The Spiral oscillates between a group orientation and individual orientation, indicated by the alternately warm and cool colors assigned to the stages. This will be apparent as we move through the next chapters. Keep these ideas in mind as you read on, and if there are unanswered questions, read more about Spiral Dynamics in the Appendix.

The vMemes of the First Tier

The First Tier of the Spiral Dynamics model consists of six vMemes (worldviews, stages) designated by six colors: BEIGE, PURPLE, RED, BLUE, ORANGE, GREEN. This First Tier is characterized by survival and accomplishments, with a "having and doing" mindset, driven by the ego and the need to make your way in the world.

BEIGE vMeme: also known as Survival, Archaic, Instinctive.

The Archaic stage is the stage of the first humans, the hunter-gatherers. This stage is pre-language and non-reflective, and as a pre-egoic stage, these earliest human beings, our first ancestors, experienced no individuality: they had no sense of separation from the natural or spirit world. They were in the Garden of Eden, so to speak. Our ancestors gradually developed their brains for about 200,000 years until they were able to be self-aware and developed the spoken word. With that, their worldview, and their vision of themselves in the world shifted dramatically.

PURPLE vMeme: Mystical, Magical, Animistic.

Basic Motive and Theme: "Blood relationship and mysticism in a magical and scary world." "Keep the spirits happy and the tribe's nest safe and warm."[13]

PURPLE Magical consciousness emerged around 40,000 years ago and was the predominant worldview for about 30,000 years. In other words, PURPLE was the only worldview from 40,000 to 8000 BCE. With newly developed speech, storytelling brought imaginative ideas of causation into these ancestors' awareness. This period saw the rise of tribes engaged in farming and animal husbandry, typically led by a shaman or spiritual leader. During this era, our ancestors populated the globe and developed social structures to the extent of building city walls.

The PURPLE consciousness appears in the earliest (pre-history) writers of the Bible. We will study this worldview and its perception of God in Chapters 4 and 5, and you can read more about PURPLE in the Appendix.

RED vMeme: Warrior, Egocentric Consciousness.

Basic Motive and Theme: "Enforce power over self, others, and nature through exploitive independence." "Be what you are and do what you want, regardless."[14] The previous stage provided safety in a time of migration and danger from outsiders, but that worldview was very limited and inadequate to handle changing life conditions. The next evolutionary impulse was to break away from the stifling group think of PURPLE's tribal mindset and make one's way in the world. The RED consciousness is assertive and creative, as illustrated by the ancient Egyptian Empire in the Bronze Age, and later, the Roman Empire. In this new frontier, which emerged around 10,000 years ago, "might makes right." The strong survive through dominating all others. This stage is like the teenager or young adult who, in many ways, appears as capable as a mature adult, but is impulsive, reactionary, and reckless.

The PURPLE and RED worldviews appear through the earliest writers of the Bible. We will study this worldview's perception of God in Chapter 5.

BLUE vMeme: Authoritarian, Mythic, Purposeful.

Basic Motive and Theme: "Absolute belief in one right way and obedience to authority" "Life has meaning, direction, and purpose, with predetermined outcomes."[15] After many thousands of years of a dominant RED Assertive, Egocentric paradigm, an Authoritarian code of conduct rose to bring order to a chaotic, unsafe world. BLUE introduced morality, duty and honor, sacrifice, and responsibility. This worldview emphasizes the community: sacrifice your personal needs now for the sake of the future of our community or nation. Most of the Hebrew Bible is written from the BLUE worldview, beginning with the era of the kings and the Hebrew prophets. These writers emphasized BLUE characteristics by outlining a new morality in the Ten Commandments; by writing detailed cultic laws about food, clothing, and feasts; and by providing eloquent verbiage to show attention to detail and awe toward God.

We will study this worldview's perception of God in Chapter 6. There is much more information about the Authoritarian BLUE vMeme in the Appendix.

ORANGE vMeme: Modern, Rationalistic, "Achievist"

Basic Motive: "Possibility thinking focused on making things better for self."[16] The Modern, Rationalistic vMeme is "I" oriented: a person prioritizes their identity over group identity. It is an adult stage of self-awareness, self-empowerment, and achievement, of reason and release of myth. This global worldview became the predominant paradigm of the Western world during The Enlightenment and continues through today to be the most powerful worldview of Western culture, although it is losing its influence because of its unhealthy behaviors. (Read more detail about all the vMemes in the Appendix)

Although ORANGE Modern vMeme didn't emerge until the 17th century CE, we can see seeds of ORANGE consciousness in the Wisdom Writings of the Bible which we will study in Chapter 7.

GREEN vMeme: Post-Modern, Relativistic, Communitarian.

Basic Theme: "Seek peace within the inner self and explore with others, the caring dimensions of community." As a response to the cold competition of the Modern Age, the Post-Modern worldview swings to community-oriented values. This is the world of sharing and caring, of giving oneself in service for the benefit of all, to create a world that works for everyone.

We see seeds of GREEN consciousness in the wisdom writers of the Bible and in Jesus' teachings, which also exhibit Second Tier consciousness.

Second Tier:

In this study of the Hebrew Scriptures, the first tier is all that we will observe. Second Tier consciousness is markedly different from the First Tier. The difference is described by the model's originator as a momentous leap because when a person shifts out of Post-Modern GREEN, they release the drive to survive, have, and do. They awaken from the bondage of ego to identify with "being." You can read more about the Second Tier in the Appendix.

Processing this Chapter:

(Numbers are for reference only and do not indicate suggested order or importance.)

1. Check your knowledge. Give a short statement of your understanding of each of the First Tier vMemes' characteristics and values, and assumptions about the world. Be sure to include all six vMemes: BEIGE, PURPLE, RED, BLUE, ORANGE, and GREEN. (Use the Appendix for more details)

2. Consider: Do you see that you have moved through each of these worldviews as you grew up? Do you feel that you might have skipped one? How can you make sense of this? How might you revisit that value system and reconcile with it? We will discuss this again in Chapter 8)

3. Remember to refer to a much more complete explanation of Spiral Dynamics in the Appendix to this book.

Chapter 3

Tool #2: The Documentary Hypothesis

For millennia, both Jewish and Christian teachings purported a myth that Moses was the sole author of the Torah (the first five books of the Hebrew Scriptures). From this myth arose a belief that the Torah was God's direct revelation to Moses. Out of this premise followed the Christian teaching that the Bible was the only revelation of God to humankind, that it was infallible and fully inspired. (2nd Timothy 3: 16)

Anyone who reads these books logically will find the one-author theory unacceptable. Why would this author have written two creation stories? Why would he contradict himself in the story of the Great Flood? Why would there be two sets of commandments? Why are there different names for God? If Moses wrote the Torah, how did he write about his own death? The informed reason and logic of the modern intellect deem such discrepancies indefensible. Many of us have shelved the Bible in exasperation over these and many more contradictions.

Almost a thousand years ago, in the eleventh century CE, a Jewish scholar named Isaac bin Yashush attempted to explain that Moses could not have written parts of the Torah. "Isaac the blunderer" was quickly quieted by a rabbi, who may have agreed, but did not want to speak out against the establishment. The rabbi wrote, "And he who understands will keep silent."[17]

Hundreds of years later, the Enlightenment dawned upon Europe, ushering in an exciting climate of scholarly logic and intellectual exploration, including independent scholarly quests for Biblical authorship. Spinoza, a brilliant philosopher of the 17th century planted a question about Moses' authorship of the Torah. The question was taken up by other scholars who looked at indicators such as linguistics, style, elaborations, and repeated phrases to determine when and by whom the work was written. Sometimes the writers referred to specific historical events, for example, the phrase, "in the twenty-second year of King so and so" helped them to determine the writer.

By the mid–1800s, after carefully synthesizing many findings about linguistics, doublets, and contradictions, and after integrating newly available archeological discoveries, extra-biblical sources, and numerous other factors, Julius Wellhausen proposed *the Documentary Hypothesis,* concluding that four distinct voices contributed to the Torah.

These four distinct voices in the Torah were given names: the Jahwist, the Elohist, the Priestly, and the Deuteronomist, in short J, E, P and D. There were redactors, editors, and revisors as well who inserted specifics like time, place, and kindred relationships. They are referred to as RJE, the redactor of the J and E writings, and R, the redactor of the P and the D writings.

Since being presented to scholars in the mid–1800s, the Documentary Hypothesis has been subject to much examination and debate. But despite its critics, for over a century no other theory has been credible enough to replace it as the most persuasive theory of Biblical authorship. The Documentary Hypothesis is taught and debated in most credible scholarly seminaries. We will use the discoveries of Richard Elliott Friedman as our compass for this study.

The Early Writers J and E

The J writer: Tenth and Ninth Centuries BCE

The Jahwist or J writer is so named because this writer refers to God as *Jahwe,* the German spelling of Yahweh or YHWH. The term Jehovah derives from *Jahwe*. The J writer ("J") identifies with Jerusalem and the southern region of Judah. Scholars agree that J most likely wrote during the prosperous reign of Solomon circa 950 BCE, but they have not determined J's specific role in society. They do agree that J was not a priest, so J could have been a woman. Friedman suggests that although the writer knew that men were in charge, women had their ways of influencing decisions. The J writer furnishes stories that include women like Sarah, Rebecca, and Rachel who wield power and influence within this male-dominated structure. Therefore, for the intrigue of it, we will use female pronouns for the J writer. J began her story at the beginning of time and finished her epic tale with the death and succession of King David. Her story can be gleaned from portions of Genesis, Exodus, and Numbers, as well as Joshua, Judges, 1st and 2nd Samuel, and 1st Kings. The J writer's entire story is presented by Friedman in his book "The Hidden Book of the Bible."

Why is the J writer's epic tale so significant? Before the earliest biblical writings, the written word was used only for trade, commerce, laws, and epic mythology, but not to narrate the social, political, and religious history of a people. Beginning her epic story with "In the day that YHWH made the earth and skies..."[18] this groundbreaking writer documents a vast narrative of generations of people chosen by YHWH. (Later referred to as "the LORD God.") With this simple decision to start at the beginning and proceed to track the story of the people that YHWH created, J displays a newly emerging worldview: she perceives that her people were moving forward into a future. Before this, the predominant worldview was cyclical: people did not sense that life was going anywhere. Like the seasons, which repeat and repeat, life was a consistent, repetitive closed cycle. There was no sense of a forward motion toward something greater, so there was no need to record the stories.

The J writer's contribution to the Hebrew Bible is the oldest known narrative that tells the story of a people. J considered the Hebrew people to be chosen to enter a covenant with the almighty, thus they placed great value on that covenant with YHWH and were aware, perhaps for the first time in global history, that they could anticipate a future. They were going somewhere. This idea becomes firmly established in the psyche of the Hebrew people and continues to shape the consciousness of the people hundreds of years later through the voice of the prophet Jeremiah: "For surely I know the plans I have for you, says the Lord, plans for your welfare and not for harm, to give you a future with hope" (Jeremiah 29: 11).

Richard Elliott Friedman's *The Hidden Book of the Bible* features the stand-alone work of the J writer. Friedman calls J's narrative "The First Prose Masterpiece" because it is a compelling and complete narrative. But, as presented in the Torah, J's epic story does not stand alone. It is intermixed with ideas and details from the E, P, and D writers.

The E Writer: Ninth and Eighth Centuries BCE

He is named Elohist or "E" because he referred to the early God as *El* (*Elohim*). Since he is idealistically loyal to the Levite priests of Shiloh, he is assumed to be male. The E writer wrote from the perspective of the northern tribes of Israel: he shows allegiance to sacred places, leaders, and customs familiar to Israel. The Documentary Hypothesis dates the E writer to the second half of the ninth century BCE, but he also might have written as late as the 700s BCE, as the nation was falling under Assyria's pressure.[19] If so, we can guess this writer was passionately dedicated to preserving the stories of Israel's heroes, although only fragments of E documents remain. Probably when Israel was destroyed in 722, refugees carried the E documents into Judah, where the Redactor (RJE) wove them into the J writings. (This is the same time as the P writer.)

The J and E Writers: At the Birth of God's Kingdom on Earth

Both J and E cover oral history going back to the birth of their people many centuries before. J begins at creation. The E writer picks up the story with Abraham and traces it similar to the J writer. Both acknowledge twelve tribes coming out of the twelve sons of Jacob. Both J and E were strongly tied to a tribal covenant with an awe-inspiring God. Both knew the stories of the conquest of Canaan and their God-fearing leaders. Both had collective memories of the wanderings in the desert under Moses' leadership. They knew this story as the road to the "land flowing with milk and honey." (Exodus 3: 8; Numbers 13: 27; Deuteronomy 26: 15 written by the J writer; Exodus 3: 17; Exodus 33: 3 by the E writer)

Around the turn of the millennium, 1000 BCE, after centuries of struggle and warfare, the people demanded a king to lead them and represent them on the world stage. (1st Samuel 8. J writer) David was a warrior tribal leader of a small city-state. King David's city-state provided relative stability and security for the people. This is most likely when the J writer wrote her masterpiece.

When J and E reported their remembrances, they structured the story through their tribal understanding. The two early writers told similar stories with different emphases, different locations, and different heroes. Friedman explains, "The J stories fit the cities and territory of Judah. The E stories fit the cities and territory of Israel."[20]

The following excerpt is a particularly good example of an intermingling of J and E. It is the story of Joseph and his jealous brothers, the twelve sons of Jacob the Patriarch. As you read it, you'll start to wonder about the details: Was it Reuben or Judah who protected Joseph's life? Did they sell their brother to the Midianites or the Ishmaelites? The answer is that it depends on who's telling the story. Consistent with their tribal identities, the J writer says it was the brother Judah who was the compassionate one, and the E writer says it was Reuben. This is one of many examples that alerted scholars to consider multiple authors.

Genesis 37:19-36 (Regular font: J writer. **Bold font: E writer.**)

[19]And the brothers said to one another, "Here comes the dream-master, that one there! And now, come on, and let's kill him and throw him in one of the pits, and we'll say a wild animal ate him, and we'll see what his dreams will be!"

[21]**And Reuben heard, and he saved him from their hand. And he said, "Let's not take his life." [22]And he said, "Don't spill blood. Throw him into this pit that's in the wilderness, and don't put out a hand against him" – in order to save him from their hand, to bring him back to his father.** [23]When Joseph came to his brothers and they took off Joseph's coat, the coat of many colors, which he had on.

[24] **And they took him and threw him into the pit. And the pit was empty; there was no water in it. [25]And they sat down to eat bread.**

And they raised their eyes and saw, and here was a caravan of Ishmaelites coming from Gilead, and their camels were carrying spices and balsam and myrrh, going to bring them down to Egypt. [26]And Judah said to his brothers, "What profit is there if we kill our brother and cover his blood? [27]Come on and let's sell him to the Ishmaelites, and let our hand not be on him, because he's our brother, our flesh." And his brothers listened.

[28]**And Midianite people, merchants passed, and they pulled and lifted Joseph from the pit.**

And the sold Joseph to the <u>Ishmaelites</u> for twenty weights of silver. And they brought Joseph to Egypt.

²⁹And Reuben came back to the pit, and here: Joseph was not in the pit. And he tore his clothes.[21]

Later Writers P and D: At the Fall of the Nations

As mentioned, the E writer wrote from Israel's point of view sometime during the sovereign state of Israel (922-722 BCE). Israel had been an unsteady tribal federation and was unable to withstand the invasion of Assyria, the ominous warrior empire to the northeast. Assyria left a wake of destruction throughout the land. The people of Israel disbursed. Some fled north, many fled south into Judah carrying E's writings with them, and others continued south into Egypt. This demographic shift resulted in the "ten lost tribes of Israel," when the ten northern tribes were gradually assimilated by other peoples and virtually disappeared from history. Many Israelites took shelter with their southern tribal cousins and assimilated into Judean culture. This is the time when the E documents migrated to Judah and other places in the diaspora. We will discuss this century again in Chapter 6 when we consider the writings of the prophets.

Judah survived Assyria's aggression by agreeing to pay them annual tributes; they became vassals to Assyria, meaning Judah was no longer a sovereign nation. The loss of their sovereign status was a major blow to the Hebrew identity, and the time was ripe for the introduction of religious devotion and reform.

The P Writer: Eighth and Seventh Centuries BCE

The P writer is named P because his focus is on priestly law. He recorded the laws that were forming in the society and contributed some details and alternative stories to the J and E events. His details focused on lineage, descriptions, measurements, locations, names, kindred relationships, the priesthood, and worship practices. P is the sole author of the poetic creation story in Genesis 1.

Judah's King Hezekiah, having witnessed the fall of Israel, (722 BCE) instituted sweeping monotheistic reforms, and provided a stable environment for thirty years, during which the P writer did his work. Hezekiah's successor Manasseh ignored many of his father's religious reforms, reintroducing "the high places" (the worship sites of Baal and Asherah). (This story is recorded in 2nd Kings 18-23.)

The D Writer: Sixth Century BCE

The D writer is credited with the Deuteronomistic Writings. "Deutero" means "second source," and D's work is indeed a second telling of the early stories, with revisions that display the reformed ideas of the sixth century. The Deuteronomist lived in the court of King Josiah, (640-609 BCE) the great-grandson of the faithful King Hezekiah, and the grandson of the unfaithful King Manasseh. Josiah established another round of monotheistic reforms and issued further societal laws. The D writer retells the history of the people with hindsight and political finesse, and with a clear concept of monotheistic theocracy. He recorded all the reforms and helped Josiah establish a renewed commitment to Hebrew law and practice centered in Jerusalem. King Josiah's reforms were backed by a conveniently "discovered" scroll of law in 622 BCE. Scholars associate the Deuteronomist as the author of this significant scroll which was read publicly to all the people every day. (We will consider more details about the D writers in Chapter 6).

Meanwhile, to the southeast the huge empire of Babylon spread westward along the river valley, swiftly conquering the region that Assyria had occupied, just north of Judah. In 586 BCE, the Babylonians destroyed Jerusalem and the beloved temple built by Solomon four hundred years before. Elite Judeans were exiled to Babylon and the common people were left to scrape out a living from the scorched countryside.

Summary of Authors and Writings

Scriptures Attributed to J, E, P, D		
Writers	Books	When Written
J: God is called Jahweh. "The First Prose Masterpiece."	Parts of Genesis, Exodus, and Numbers. Parts of Joshua, Judges, 1 and 2 Samuel, and 1 Kings 2, through the death of David.	10th and 9th Centuries BCE
E: God is called Elohim.	Parts of Genesis, Exodus, Numbers, and some verses in Deuteronomy.	9th and 8th Centuries BCE
P is the Priestly source.	Genesis 1, details inserted throughout J's narrative, Exodus 25-40, all of Leviticus; most of Numbers, and one verse in Deuteronomy.	8th and 7th Centuries BCE
D: the Deuteronomistic School	Chapters 1-30 of Deuteronomy, plus parts of the Deuteronomistic History: Parts of Joshua, Judges, Samuel, Kings, and Jeremiah.	6th Century BCE
Redactors	The Redactor wove the stories together and added additions to the text. He also assembled the Psalms.	8th through 5th Centuries BCE

This knowledge about the authorship of the Bible can clarify some confusing Biblical discrepancies. Here and in the following chapters, we will examine three Biblical mysteries that can be understood using the information provided by The Documentary Hypothesis.

Example 1: Two Creation Myths by J and P

If you start reading the Bible in the very beginning, you will stumble upon the first big contradiction: the creation story. There are two different creation stories in Genesis 1 and 2. So, let's compare them. First, we notice their commonality: both assume that God was present and was the catalyst at the beginning of time. The phrase "In the beginning, God" is the foundation of religious faith. God has been the dreamer and instigator of the universe, the earth, and all beings on the earth. Similarly, neither of these stories attempts to define God, and both see God as an absolute, timeless presence.

Read the creation story in Genesis 2:4b-25. This is the first creation story written, and J is the author (tenth century BCE). J's writing is a straightforward narrative without commentary or explanations. It has mystical reverence for the creator who is a caring, attentive, people-oriented god. J displays a highly anthropomorphized creator whose process is childly impulsive and endearing. We will revisit J's creation myth in Chapter 5.

Next, read the creation story in Genesis 1: 1 through 2: 3. The P writer wrote this story most likely in the eighth century BCE. In reading P's creation story, we can sense a more elegant writing style, a poetic lilt to the phrases, and a more transcendent god. We will revisit P's creation myth in Chapter 6.

Example 2: The Great Flood by J and P

The Great Flood is an ominous early collective memory, recorded in many different ancient cultures. The Biblical writers perceived that such a catastrophe must have happened because God was unhappy with His creation. The story is documented by J and P, written centuries apart. If you read the stories separately, you'll see that the J and P writers originally wrote complete stories appropriate for their stages of consciousness. The Redactors did not cut out conflicting detail. They intricately interlaced these two versions of the Great Flood, switching back and forth fourteen times. It can be confusing to read the text without knowing there were two writers. Read the following sections, keeping in mind that two different writers are at work.

(**Bold** indicates J is the writer. *Italics* indicate P is the writer.)

Genesis 6: **5-8,** *9b-23*
Genesis 7: **1-5, 7,** *8-9,* **10,** *11,* **12,** *13-16a,* **16b-20,** *21,* **22-23,** *24*
Genesis 8: *1-2a,* **2b-3a,** *3b-5,* **6,** *7,* **8-12,** *13a,* **13b,** *14-19,* **20-22**
Genesis 9: *1-17,* **18-27**

Example 3: The Ten Commandments by J and D

There are two different lists of commandments in the Torah. The J writer (Exodus 34) gives a list of ten ancient tribal laws appropriate for a nomadic tribal society. The later writer D adds the famous "Thou shalt not" concepts of morality and ethics. (Deuteronomy 5 and Exodus 20, which duplicate the commandments of Deuteronomy 5, but do not appear to belong to any of the four major sources.) [22]

Two creation myths, two accounts of the Great Flood, and two sets of commandments: We will revisit these three discrepancies in later chapters and notice their contrasting worldviews.

Two Sets of Commandments	
The J writer: Tenth Century BCE Exodus 34	The D writer Seventh Century BCE Deuteronomy 5 (and Exodus 20)
1. Worship no other god.	1. Have no other gods before YHWH.
2. Make no covenant with aliens.	2. Make no idols.
3. Make no cast idols.	3. Keep the sabbath holy.
4. Keep the feast of unleavened bread.	4. Do not use God's name wrongly.
5. Give firstborn to YHWH.	5. Honor father and mother.
6. Work six days, rest on the seventh day.	6. Do not murder.
7. Observe the feast of weeks.	7. Do not commit adultery.
8. Don't mix sacrificial blood with leaven.	8. Do not steal.
9. Give first fruits to YHWH.	9. Do not bear false witness.
10. Don't boil a kid goat in its mother's milk.	10. Do not covet a neighbor's house or wife or other property.

Processing This Chapter

1. Check your knowledge. Over what periods were the Hebrew Scriptures written? How do we know that? Explain the name, and approximate dates of the four writers of the Torah: J, E, P, D.

2. Consider the different lenses with which we can read the Bible. What kind of lens is the Documentary Hypothesis? As you engage in this course, are you willing to stretch your viewpoint so that you can experience the evolutionary lens?

3. Reflect. For some readers, the implications of the Documentary Hypothesis can cause a ripple of emotion: surprise, shock, anger, or a crisis of faith. Others might feel relief or satisfaction that their hunch about the book is backed by scholars. Consider that this scholarly information might not have been shared with the people of faith because it would indeed rock their faith. Process this in your journal or your discussion group. Continue to observe your emotional and spiritual response throughout the reading of this book.

4. Consider. How does the information provided by the Documentary Hypothesis affect your impression or beliefs about the church? Consider why Christianity has not disseminated this information: Are ministers afraid they'd lose their jobs if they spoke so boldly? Have ministers tried to share the information and been denied opportunities by the very people who could benefit from it? Have church members resisted hearing this information? Perhaps, out of compassion for the people and honoring the tradition, ministers have chosen to perpetuate the mythic theology than present reason-based information that could upset the congregants. Is this study considered too detailed for the" lay person," thus perpetuating the secret? As we study the Spiral, come back to this question, and reflect again.

5. Learn more. With deep gratitude to Richard Elliott Friedman, I highly recommend further study on the Documentary Hypothesis. These books have been at my side throughout the writing of this book.

    •   *Who Wrote the Bible?* (1987). Friedman explains the details of his findings and includes an extensive chart indicating who authored each verse of the Torah.
    •   *The Hidden Book of the Bible* (1999). Friedman consolidates the J writer's storyline called the "First Prose Masterpiece,"

embedded in the Torah, Joshua, Judges, 1st and 2nd Samuel, and 1st Kings 2:1-34, up to the death of David.

- *The Bible with Sources Revealed* (2005). Friedman translates the Torah in its entirety, identifying each author (J, E, P, D) using colored fonts.

Chapter 4:

A Magical God: PURPLE vMeme in the Bible

"As they journeyed, a terror from God fell upon the
cities all around them, so that no one pursued them."
(Genesis 35:5; E writer).

Although writers **J** and E lived at a time when the RED
'Impulsive' worldview was well-established and BLUE
'Purposeful' was emerging, they recorded the stories of their ancestors,
and in doing so conveyed some ideas that had been included in
PURPLE consciousness. Their written stories are a precious treasure
to the modern reader: a window into the collective consciousness of
more than 10,000 years ago!

The PURPLE Tribal, Magical Animistic worldview is nicknamed
"KinSpirits"[23] because it reflects the "we" tribal clan society with a
chief in the lead, often a shaman. The tribe's primary function was to
survive, and its members had learned that they could thrive in a tight
tribal system. This pre-rational worldview was attuned to and would
make sense of natural events through stories involving spirits. This
is a time of meager language skills, artistic rituals and symbols, and a
mystical understanding of dreams and signs. Refer to the Appendix
for more information about the PURPLE worldview.

Historical Context--"Pre-History"

The Bible stories about creation, Adam, and Eve, Cain and Abel, and the patriarchs (Abraham, Isaac, and Jacob), as well as the stories of the Exodus and the wandering through the wilderness allegedly occurred long before someone wrote them down. Although they are perhaps not fact, they are valuable to explain the Jewish identity. This era is dubbed the Patriarchal Period. If historical, Abraham, the "father of Judaism," is said to have migrated from Ur, a city at the mouth of the Euphrates River, to Canaan around the time that Ur collapsed (1950 BCE). Abraham's tribe would have arrived in Canaan around 1900 BCE.

Perception of the World through the PURPLE Lens in the Hebrew Scriptures

In a PURPLE worldview, the focus is on maintaining a kinship social structure, developing communication skills, and awakening to early cause-and-effect thinking. The tribe is their only identity: their relationship with each other is not individualized, and social behavior is clan focused. Good and evil are defined as: good is that which helps the group; evil is that which threatens the group's survival. The J and E writers gave us stories that display a tribal group-think culture, including the us-them mentality, societal shunning, and ritual displays of appeasement. (Read more about PURPLE in the Appendix)

Characteristics/Values of PURPLE Tribal, Magical in the early Biblical writers:

- "We" tribal identity, "us versus them." KinSpirits
- Mysticism in a magical and scary world.
- Sacred places and items
- Spirits, Mediums, Divination, Dream interpretation

- Intuitive, attuned to nature and nuances.
- Obedience to the spirits and mystical signs; rituals, traditions, symbols
- Superstitions, guardian angels, blood oaths.
- Talking animals

Tribal identity; Us versus Them; Fear of Outside Tribes. The early writers of the Hebrew Bible dealt with the fear of any outside tribe. We find these tribes listed in several places in Genesis, most of them were ancient relatives. The only tribes included as true Israelites and therefore the only ones they could trust were those descended from Noah's son, Shem, and later from the tribe of Israel.

Sacred Places and Altars. There are many mentions of people setting up piles of stones to indicate sacred places. These are recorded by the J and E writers, exclusively.

Noah built an altar in gratitude after the flood, indicating an early practice of making altars. "Then Noah built an altar to the LORD and took of every clean animal and every clean bird and offered burnt offerings on the altar." (Genesis 8:20 J writer)

Jacob built an altar to mark his experience of the presence of God: "And he was afraid, and said, 'How awesome is this place! This is none other than the house of God, and this is the gate of skies.' And Jacob got up early in the morning and took the stone that he had set as his headrest and set it as a pillar and poured oil on its top." (Genesis 28:17-18, E writer)[24].

Jacob had a complicated relationship with his father-in-law, Laban, that was made even more complicated because the story is a weaving of J and E's writings. Jacob had married two of Laban's daughters (Leah and Rachel) causing tension between the families. After much disagreement and discussion, they made a covenant to respect each other, and they set up a pile of stones to bear witness (Genesis 31:45–53, E writer).

Jacob and Esau reconcile after decades of estrangement, and they set up an altar at that place naming it "El, God of Israel." (Genesis 33: 20 E writer)[25]

Magic. When YHWH appointed Moses to represent Him, Moses wondered if the people and Pharoah would believe him. YHWH gave Moses a powerful sign of His presence. He told Moses to throw his staff to the ground. When Moses threw it down it became a snake! Then YHWH told Moses to pick the snake up by its tail, and the snake turned back into a staff. YHWH told Moses this was "so that they may believe that the LORD the God of their ancestors, the God of Abraham, the God of Isaac, and the God of Jacob, has appeared to you." (Exodus 4: 4 E writer)

Spirits and Mediums. The peoples' fear of the power of their prophets (and the prophets' gods) also shows up in the Bible. In two "J" stories, we see a fear of the prophet Samuel's god. In another story, King Saul asks a medium to call Samuel forth from the other side, and Saul is afraid. "I will call unto the LORD, and he shall send thunder and rain; that you may perceive and see that your wickedness is great... [18] So Samuel called unto the LORD, and the LORD sent thunder and rain that day: and all the people greatly feared the LORD and Samuel." (1 Samuel 12:17-18. J writer).

King Saul, the first king of Israel/Judah, expelled the mediums and wizards from the kingdom. But after his advisor Samuel died, Saul needed some counsel regarding the threat of the Philistines, so he sought advice from a medium. He disguised himself and went to a medium who was able to "bring up" Samuel (1 Samuel 28, J writer).

Divination, Omens, Curses, and Blessings. "Come now, curse this people for me, since they are stronger than I; perhaps I shall be able to defeat them and drive them from the land; for I know that whomever you bless is blessed, and whomever you curse is cursed. So, the elders of Moab and the elders of Midian departed with the fees for divination in their hand; and they came to Balaam and gave him Balak's message. (Numbers 22: 6-7a, E writer).

"Balaam saw that it pleased the Lord to bless Israel, so he did not go, as at other times, to look for omens, but set his face toward the wilderness." (Numbers 24: 1. E writer)

Sacred Icons. While Moses was on the mountain getting instructions from YHWH, the people became restless and wondered if Moses would return. They wanted to keep traveling, and they believed they needed the blessing and protection of the gods. Aaron collected all the gold from the Israelites (rings and earrings), melted them down, and cast the gold into an image of a calf. (Exodus 32, E writer). The calf was the symbol of the local god, Baal, as well as a divine symbol in Egypt and Mesopotamia.

Sacred Items. The ark of the covenant was a portable wooden box covered with pure gold, inside and out that contained three sacred objects: the stone tablets containing the commandments, Aaron's rod, and a pot of manna. It traveled with the people into the promised land and was given a sacred space in the tabernacle. During the "conquest of Canaan," the ark was carried into battle and subsequently stolen by enemies. But each enemy that held the ark encountered sudden inexplicable tragic deaths. It became a thing of fear, representing the power of YHWH. (Read how the ark helped win battles for the Israelites and struck fear in the hearts of their enemies in 1st Samuel chapters 4-6 by the J writer). The P writer described the artistic details of the ark centuries later. The description is influenced by Egyptian culture. (Exodus 25:10-22 P writer.)

Dream Interpretation. This stage of awareness believes that dreams are messages from the spirit world. And they are interpreted by a man of God. Example: Jacob is on his way to meet his estranged brother, Esau. On his journey, he slept one night with a rock as his pillow. He dreamt of a ladder reaching up to the skies, with angels ascending and descending. He was struck with the awe of his experience and knew that God was in that place. (Genesis 28:12 E writer)

Another example: Joseph interprets dreams: "When Joseph came to them in the morning, he saw that they were troubled. So, he asked them, 'Why are your faces downcast today?' They said to him, 'We have had dreams, and there is no one to interpret them.' And Joseph said to them, 'Do not interpretations belong to God? Please tell them to me.'" (Genesis 40: 6-8, E writer).

Joseph interprets Pharoah's Dreams of Feast and Famine (Genesis 41: 1-57 E writer)

Talking Animals. The early myth includes stories about animals that can talk. They seem to be what we might call "our inner dialogue," but at the PURPLE Magical stage of consciousness, with no self-awareness, a storyteller might consider that the source of the thought was a nearby animal. In the Garden of Eden myth, we meet the animal who is "craftier than any other wild animal that YHWH had made." The serpent challenged the woman by asking, "Did God say...?" The serpent became a powerful, fearful totem. (Genesis 3:1, J writer).

Another talking animal story is the one about Balaam and his donkey. Balaam travels with his donkey and they encounter an angel on the road that only the donkey can see. The donkey continually balks and refuses to go forward. Balaam, unable to see the angel, beats the donkey three different times. After the third occurrence, the donkey speaks aloud and asks why Balaam stuck him three times. Not surprised that the donkey talked, Balaam converses with the donkey. A moment later the E writer tells us, "YHWH uncovered Balaam's eyes, and he saw the angel of YHWH standing up in the road, and his sword drawn in his hand, And he knelt and bowed to his nose." (Numbers 22:31. E writer)[26]. This story displays a God that performs supernatural events: God works through angels and donkeys. The event occurs three times, indicating a ritual that is an attribute of PURPLE consciousness. This interesting story fills three chapters. (Numbers 22-24, E writer).

Animal Magic. While the people were in the wilderness, they complained of their misery to Moses. As a result of this disobedience, God sent "fiery" snakes (poisonous) that bit the people, and many died. The people, being sorry for complaining, begged Moses to send the snakes away. After Moses prayed for the people, YHWH instructed him on what to do. Moses made a serpent out of bronze and put it up on a pole so that a person who got a snake bite could look up at the bronze serpent and live (Numbers 21, E writer). (This story is full of literary symbology.)

Perception of God through the PURPLE Mystical, Magical Lens

The PURPLE worldview assigns key characteristics to the God in the Bible: anthropomorphic, polytheistic, magical, and mighty and demanding sacrifices.

Like the toddler who has no systematic reasoning skills, the PURPLE worldview sees the world as enchanted, responds to events with wonder and fear, and makes sense of natural phenomena by attributing them to a god or magic.

Anthropomorphic. PURPLE's idea of God is an immanent[27] anthropomorphized being who talks with humans through animals, burning bushes, and storms and is the source of natural phenomena. Both the J and the E writers reveal a PURPLE magical perception of a God who is responsible for all the mysteries of life. They wrote stories to portray an imminent, personable creator. In Genesis 3, J writes "And they hear the sound of the Lord God walking in the garden at the time of the evening breeze..." (Genesis 3: 8a) creating an image of a God walking in the garden, calling out for the man, and making clothes for the man and woman. This God is not perceived to be omniscient (all-knowing) as he cannot find the two humans he had placed in the garden. In Genesis Chapters 5-9, the J writer describes a very personal God who builds the ark, puts Noah and his family in it, and closes the door personally. After the flood, He opens the door and lets them out. Noah makes a sacrifice, and this very human-like God is pleased with the pleasant odor.

During the escape from Egypt, God delivers the people out of Egypt, crossing the Reed Sea: "YHWH drove back the sea with a strong east wind all night and turned the sea into the dry ground" (Exodus 14:21, J writer).

Polytheistic. Typically, the PURPLE consciousness supports polytheism. The J writer reports that YHWH refers to itself as "we" and "us." J might have believed that YHWH was a plural being or a group of gods. In the story about the tower of Babel, God talked to the others: "And YHWH said, "Come now let us go down and confuse their language..." (Genesis 11:7, J writer). YHWH wanted to confuse the language of the people so they could not understand each other and do things that were reserved for the gods.

Mystical experiences of the divine. PURPLE attributes all phenomena and natural events (thunder and lightning, high winds, phases of the moon) to the actions of the spirits. This worldview centers on visions, superstitions, divinations, and rituals. The PURPLE consciousness believes it must appease the gods and goddesses through rituals and sacrifice, to receive health remedies and a successful hunt.

The early writers record their ancient myths in a language that is true to their pre-rational worldview. They identify places, animals, and natural events as spiritual, connecting the landmarks to the story of the Patriarchs. These PURPLE-consciousness stories did not question that God made a bush burn without being consumed and caused water to spring from desert rocks. In an interweaving of J and E writings, Exodus 3-4 demonstrates that the writers valued the use of magic to convey the awe and fear of their God. A belief in magic is a healthy characteristic in PURPLE as it indicates the use of the imagination to create things not already obvious.

Magic to Prove YHWH's power:

The E writer tells us that YHWH brought plagues upon the population of Egypt. When Moses and Aaron stood in front of Pharaoh, God said, "I will send all my plagues upon you, and upon your officials, and upon your people, so that you may know that there is no one like me in all the earth" (Exodus 9:14, E writer). E's story continues for several chapters. (Exodus 7–10)

Plagues listed by the E writer: The Nile River is turned into blood, and frogs, gnats, flies, and locusts invade the city. Egypt's livestock die. Hail, thunder, and fire come down from the sky, and darkness "that can be felt" enveloped the population for three days. (Exodus 10:21)

The magic continues in the wilderness where, according to the story, Moses and his people camped. YHWH went in front of the Israelites in a column of clouds by day and a column of fire at night to lead them through the desert (Exodus 13:21–22, J writer). When the people had nothing to eat, God magically provided manna to appear each day in the wilderness (Exodus 16:4, J writer). They had no water, but Moses struck a rock and water came out of it (Exodus 17: 6, E writer).

At another time, Moses' sister Miriam turns leprous by an act of God. Then God heals her after seven days in another magical act. Moses' siblings, Miriam, and Aaron were at his side while he led the Israelites through the wilderness. At one point, the siblings mumbled against Moses. YHWH showed up in a pillar of cloud and confronted them: "'Why were you not afraid to speak against my servant Moses?' . . . When the cloud went away from over the tent, Miriam had become leprous, as white as snow. . ... Then Aaron said to Moses, 'Oh, my lord, do not punish us for a sin that we have so foolishly committed. . ... And Moses cried to the Lord, 'O God, please heal her.' . . . The Lord said to Moses, 'Let her be shut out of the camp for seven days, and after that, she may be brought in again.'" (Numbers 12: 5-15, E writer).

Sacrifices appease the gods. The early writers spoke of sacrificial rituals to appease their mysterious fear-inspiring God. One significant example is the story of Abraham's sacrifice. God (Elohim) tells Abraham to sacrifice his precious late-in-life son Isaac. Abraham, obeying, took Isaac up the mountain. There he bound Isaac and laid him on the altar. E does not provide an "out" for Abraham, stating that Abraham (without Isaac) "went back to his boys"[28] (Genesis 22:1-10 and 16-19, E writer). Centuries later, the Redactor added verses 11-15, where an angel of YHWH interrupts the act and provides a ram for the sacrifice. The Redactor seemed to have perceived human sacrifice as repugnant and added the way out for Abraham.[29] Seen from a developmental perspective, knowing that centuries later a redactor wanted to soften the story helps us see a breakthrough in spiritual consciousness: a move toward rejecting the practice of human sacrifice. This is evidence of the huge shift from PURPLE (human sacrifice) to RED (animal sacrifice). Read about Abraham leading up to the sacrifice of his son Isaac for yourself (Genesis 20:1a-28; Genesis 29:6, 8-33 Genesis 22:1-10 and 16-19, E writer).

The concept of sacrificing animals continued into the RED and BLUE worldview. The Bible provides many other references to this common ritual. We will read about the human sacrifice of a virgin daughter in the next chapter. But the Blue vMeme was emerging, and the P writer would soon set stringent limits and qualifications on the ritual of sacrifice that was offered to the god to appease one's guilt for wrongdoing. (Often called the "guilt offering.")

Seeds of Consciousness

Throughout the Hebrew Bible, we come across isolated snippets, splashes, or "seeds" of consciousness that stand out because they are not present in the predominant consciousness of the time. For example, during the patriarchal period when the Tribal, Magical worldview was predominant, several stories are recorded that reveal a consciousness that has hints of the Post-Modern GREEN worldview.

The story of Patriarch Jacob and his twin brother Esau is our first example. Jacob and Esau are favored by different parents. Esau, the first born, who is entitled to the greater portion of the family inheritance, is favored by his father Isaac. Rebekah favors Jacob. She arranges for Jacob to trick his old and blind father into performing the ritual that will allow Jacob to be the prime inheritor. When Esau learns of the deceit, he vows to kill Jacob.

With the help of his mother, Jacob flees to the country of his mother's brother before Esau can kill him. He is away for a long time, long enough to marry two women and have quite a few children. The day comes when God advises Jacob in a vision to go back and face his brother. He fearfully obeys, bringing with him gifts of wealth, animals, and slaves to offer Esau recompense. On the way, Jacob has a vision in which he wrestles with an angel and is assured God is with him. The encounter did not calm Jacob's fears. He still has no reason to believe that Esau will not kill him in revenge, so he approaches with great caution. Jacob is surprised to find Esau embracing him and forgiving him. This response resembles Post-Modern GREEN values. These "seeds of consciousness" could be considered a divine inspiration or intuition that the writers heard from within (Genesis 25-27; Genesis 32, J writer).

The story of Joseph and his brothers is another example of how seeds of consciousness from another worldview appear within a prior one. This story is the longest account of any of the Patriarch stories and has many intriguing facets. Two different accounts of the story are scattered through the chapters, Genesis 39–45, told by J and E, with the details woven together within the same chapters.

Joseph is Jacob's favorite son. He is young and ambitious, with dreams of grandeur that later come true. He has one full brother, Benjamin, both born of Rachel, and ten jealous half-brothers. The ten half-brothers are away herding sheep when Jacob, their father, tells Joseph to take them some supplies. They see him coming and scheme to get revenge. When Joseph arrives, they throw him in a pit while they argue about what to do with him. Reuben or Judah (depending on which writer tells the story) argues to spare Joseph's life while the others want to kill him.

Meanwhile, a caravan of traders arrives, so the brothers either leave him in the pit or sell him to the traders. Joseph ends out in Egypt. "And YHWH was with Joseph. He was a successful man; he was in the house of his Egyptian master." Genesis 39:2. J writer) Over time, Joseph is favored by the ruling Pharaoh, then thrown in prison due to a scandalous false accusation. Yet, due to his gift of interpreting dreams (which had gotten him in trouble with his brothers), he is released and becomes second in command to the Pharaoh himself.

After many years, the brothers are forced by a famine in the land of Canaan to come to Egypt to buy grain. They must appear before Joseph, the magistrate who decides whether or not to sell them grain. They do not recognize Joseph, but he recognizes them. After putting them through some difficult tests, Joseph breaks the pretense and confesses his identity. He offers full forgiveness and then brings his whole family to Egypt where he gives them some land of their own (Genesis 37 and 39–45, J and E writers).

In a time when sons, brothers, and fathers plot and execute their kin to gain ruling power, the sentiment of forgiveness is much ahead of its time resembling post-modern Green values.

Don't Skip This Section! Interesting thoughts, anecdotes, and prompts for discussion.

(numbers are for reference only and do not indicate suggested order or importance.)

1. Who's Who in the Hebrew Scriptures: If you come across characters you don't recognize, check out this site: http://practicallymetaphysical.com/index.php/overview-hebrew-scriptures/bible-outline-hebrew-scriptures/

2. It was at the emergence of the PURPLE ᵛMeme that humankind began to engage in self-reflection. This was an awakening of consciousness: our ancestors began to be aware of thoughts; to "know that we know," and we began to question. Referring to this awakening, Ken Wilber suggests that "Adam and Eve were not thrown out of the Garden. They grew up and walked out."[30] Read Genesis 3: 4-7, (written by J), to understand the context of Wilber's claim. It includes "the tree of the knowledge of good and evil." How does this inform your thoughts about the evolution of consciousness during the PURPLE awakening?

3. Reflect: Toward the end of the PURPLE vMeme, as RED emerged, humankind began to engage in self-reflection and individualization. This was an awakening of consciousness; our ancestors began to be aware of thoughts, to "know that we know," and began to question. Reflect on the story of the man and woman being thrown out of the Garden of Eden as a result of their sin of eating from 'the tree of the knowledge of good and evil.' How can this story depict the shift from PURPLE to RED vMeme? Read Genesis 3:4-7 by the J writer.

4. Go deeper: A toddler can be confused by appearances and thoughts. He might be pretending with an adult, acting out the story of the three little pigs, and he can suddenly become frightened by the wolf, even though he knows it's a friendly adult pretending to be the big bad wolf. At this stage of brain development, the toddler has a difficult time differentiating real from imagined. Project that awareness into our ancient ancestors, who were just waking up to "thought." Process how a talking snake and donkey might make sense at that level of consciousness.

5. Apply: "Transcend and Include" is a term we use often when we discuss the evolution of consciousness. As we expand our worldview, we carry forward what is healthy from the previous stages. Do you see any healthy or unhealthy values

and characteristics of PURPLE in your understanding of the world? Of yourself? Of your spiritual practice? Of your interpretation of the human experience? Which characteristics would you like to nurture within your spiritual practice? See Chapter 3 for a list of healthy and unhealthy PURPLE values.

6. Learn more about the names of God: The early writers recognized YHWH as Israel's God. The images of YHWH in the Hebrew scriptures are very similar to the Canaanite "El" which E and P wrote about. El had a wife, Asherah, and son, Ba'al, and a daughter Anat. Ba'al meant "lord," or "master," and was represented by a bull or ram. His consort was the goddess Asherah was represented by a tall pole. (Beelzebub is associated with the god *Baal*. In Christianity, this word became synonymous with Satan.) Mid-way through the Second Temple Period the worship of YHWH alone was established. Watch an excerpt of a lecture by Professor Christine Hayes of Yale University: *The Stolen Canaanite Gods of Hebrews/Israelites: El, Baal, Asherah* June 19, 2012, 4:45 https://youtu.be/ADikz5rAjJU

7. Snow-white Miriam: The story about Miriam turning leprous is particularly disconcerting to feminists. If both siblings grumbled about Moses' superior status with YHWH, then why didn't Aaron turn leprous too? Notice the symbolism of the shape of God in this story which depicts a rather masculine Purple/RED worldview. (Numbers 12:1-14. E writer).

8. Fiction: Learn more about the PURPLE tribal mindset through two wonderful works of historical fiction. Anita Diamant in her book *The Red Tent*, reveals the traditions and challenges of the tribal women which suggest aspects of a PURPLE Tribal society. Jean Auel produced her first in a series called *The Clan of the Cave Bear*, an epic work of prehistoric fiction depicting early human tribal society.

Chapter 5:

A Warrior God: the RED vMeme in the Bible

"An eye for an eye, a tooth for a tooth" (Exodus 21:23, E writer).

In the J and E accounts of the settlement of Canaan, YHWH is a masculine warrior who leads the tribal warriors into victory, causes other armies to retreat, and demands loyalty in return. In the stories about the newly established monarchy, the hero King David's city-state is laden with egocentric impulsivity that expects personal loyalty and holds sacred a man's vow. These stories accurately characterize the RED "Impulsive" vMeme. This vMeme has the emotional maturity of a teenager: impulsive, egocentric, and unable to anticipate the consequences of their actions. It is an individualistic, independent, self-determination stage that thinks of the world as a "battleground." Its slogans include survival of the fittest; "might makes right;" dominate so others won't dominate you. Spiral Dynamics nicknamed it "PowerGods."[31]

RED is also the vMeme that develops the first glimpses of self-reflection as seen in Egyptian poetry and portraiture, as well as advancements in technology, structured armies, and roadways, because RED is motivated to protect, advance, and exploit. (Refer to the Appendix for more information about the RED vMeme.)

Historical Context

For thousands of years, during the Bronze Age, Egypt was the dominant power in the region, boasting of aggressive dynasties with a strong army. In the 1500s BCE, Egypt's territory stretched south into today's Sudan and northward into the Levant (Canaan). (The Levant is defined as the land that borders the eastern shore of the Mediterranean Sea, now inhabited by Israel, Lebanon, part of Syria, and western Jordan.)

As mentioned, the healthy RED worldview of the time was the classic Egyptian poetry and art, innovations, and trade throughout the entire Mediterranean region. The construction of the Temple is also evidence of healthy red/BLUE.

Thirteenth--Twelfth Centuries BCE

The thirteenth-century BCE was the final burst of glory in Egypt's Bronze Age. At that time, it held power over the Levant, using it as a thoroughfare of trade. It had no problem controlling the people of Canaan with just a small unit of Egyptian officials.[32] This would be the time when the Hebrew people would have escaped Egypt and migrated east into the "wilderness." But there is no evidence and no data of a mass of Israelites migrating northward or eastward into the Levant. The coastal roadway into the Levant was dotted with Egyptian inspection stations that recorded nothing about a huge mass of people traveling through the area.

Very suddenly, in just a few decades, during the twelfth-century BCE, the Bronze Age came to a full stop. There is no single just one reason why this happened. A series of changes in life conditions occurred: Geographically, there were earthquakes, a crippling period of drought, and air pollution from volcanos. Politically, warriors called "Sea Peoples" invaded Egypt several times. (Egypt is said to have captured the "Sea Peoples" and settled them into the area south of the Levant, east of the Nile. They could be the Philistines.[33]) The established worldview was facing chaos and couldn't adjust to such immense change. Climate change and invasion disrupted trade relations, which caused economic instability and political unrest. For the first time in history, the working class staged a strike. Egypt's mighty power swiftly receded, leaving the Levant with no centralized authority and in chaos. People scrambled to take hold of new opportunities, claim land, and build a life. The result was unchecked, unabated aggression. A warrior "cowboy mentality" aristocracy rose.[1] This is the context within which the Israelite identity was established.

Eleventh--Tenth Centuries BCE

As Egypt's presence faded from the Levant, the tribal people of the region experienced threats from all sides. The twelve tribes of Israel were among many nomadic tribes that were in conflict continually. This was a time of holy war. "Arise, YHWH, may your enemies be scattered and those who hate you run for their lives before you." (Numbers 10:35, J writer). Each tribe followed a leader, called a "judge," who served as a military and civic leader, mentioned, but not clearly defined in the books of Judges, 1 Samuel and Chronicles. The warfare that the J writer described in Judges and 1 Samuel is typical of this

---

[1]

period.[34] This is a pivotal period for the Levant. It sets the background for the Biblical stories of the "conquest of Canaan."

The people known as the Philistines (possibly linked to the "Sea Peoples") were a major threat to the safety of the people living in the Levant. The Philistines are described as "giants," with Goliath as their front man (1 Samuel 17, J writer). The J writer tells about the Philistines raiding and capturing the ark of the covenant but were struck with a plague and fearfully returned the ark to the Israelites with their guilt offerings (1 Samuel 6, J writer). Constantly ready against attack, jumping into battles for revenge and honor is a fear-filled way to live, which creates a fearful, victim orientation in the collective consciousness. Karen Armstrong reflects: "When the troops set out, the judge called upon YHWH to accompany the Ark. Living constantly poised against attack, and ready for war, the beleaguered people developed an embattled cult."[35]

One effect of the fall of the Bronze Age was mass migration. The Levant experienced a population boom, rising to perhaps 80,000 people in Israel. This population was too large for effective leadership under a tribal structure. By around 1000 BCE, the people expressed a desire for a centralized government and a king. They wanted someone who they could trust to lead them.

The Tenth Century BCE.

Although the Biblical Kings Saul and David are well-known, the only information we have about them is from the Bible's early Hebrew myth recorded by the J writer. No other sources acknowledge them as kings.

They were more likely tribal leaders, governing a small but growing population. But since this era is critical to the Hebrew story, it does not matter if the information about them is myth or fact. The estimated dates of the reigns of the early kings are Saul, 1020-1000; David, 1000-962; Solomon, 961-922 BCE. This is the century of the J writer, who was located in Jerusalem in Judah, as were the kings.

Political Division

The Biblical myth celebrates David as a great warrior hero, and his center of governance is a shining jewel in the desert. His son Solomon is said to have built the temple, the first permanent home for YHWH, and the masterpiece of Solomon's reign. It is said that he employed many workers for its construction and established a centralized priestly team for its maintenance. In reality, David's Jerusalem was a tiny Middle Eastern market town. His son Solomon succeeded him, and they managed to secure about one hundred years of stability amidst a time of restlessness throughout the region. David decreed a northern priestly order and a southern priestly order, which helped the people make sacrifices locally.

Solomon's attempt to centralize the priesthood in Jerusalem which is in the southern region of Judah insulted the northern tribes and their priests, who chose to govern without the leadership of Jerusalem's priests effectively splitting state and religion for the first time in Israel's history. Solomon had dishonored the priests of the northern regions. This grave political misstep contributed to civil unrest, which grew into tribal battles which split the monarchy in 922 BCE, only about 80 years after it had been created. The tribes of Judah and Benjamin in the south called themselves Judah; Jerusalem remained the capital. The ten tribes in the north called themselves Israel; Shechem and, later, Samaria became their capital.

"One kingdom—-the kingdom of Israel—-was born in the fertile valleys and rolling hills of northern Israel and grew to be among the richest, most cosmopolitan, and most powerful in the region. Today it is almost totally forgotten, except for the villainous role it plays in the biblical books of Kings. The other kingdom—the kingdom of Judah—arose in the rocky, inhospitable southern hill country. It survived by maintaining its isolation and fierce devotion to its Temple and royal dynasty. These two kingdoms represent two sides of ancient Israel's experience, two quite different societies with different attitudes and national identities."[36]

This geographical, political, and religious division is likely the reason for the discrepancies found in the different accounts of the two early authors, J, and E. The E writer lived in the northern region of Israel and spoke from the perspective of an Israelite. The J writer was from Judah in the south and told his story through the eyes of a Judean. When they told their stories, they would use locations and heroes that were relevant to their tribe or clan. Each would claim that a certain phenomenon occurred within their nation's context. When J reports the births of Jacob's sons, he focuses on Judah. When E tells the story, he focuses on the sons who fathered the northern tribes. Yet they were of the same Abrahamic ancestry.

Perception of the World through the RED Lens in the Hebrew Scriptures

The fall of the Bronze Age and the drastic changes in Life Conditions just described ended the RED empire of Egypt and paved the way for the BLUE Authoritarian vMeme to emerge in the Middle East. But, of course, the RED value system didn't lose its influence overnight. It continued as BLUE's influence rose. We can see this RED worldview in the stories about the "conquest of Canaan," and we will continue to see RED values alive for centuries to come.

In a RED Egocentric, Warrior worldview, the focus is on making sure you can conquer the odds and make it in this world, similar to the culture of a mafia family, a street gang, or a citizen militia group.

Developmentally, RED is the first stage of self-awareness. Before this, the individual was not differentiated from any other member. This stage has the zeal and fearlessness to break away and make one's way in the world. The concepts of good and evil are similar to PURPLE, (what serves the tribe is good, what threatens the tribe is evil) but it is turned toward self, not the community: what serves me is good. What threatens me is evil.

Characteristics/Values of RED Warrior, Egocentric seen in the early Biblical writers:

- "I" Individualistic; power self; Masculine orientation. PowerGods[37]
- Exploits and manipulates; honors only their own group.
- Impulsive; Self-Serving: acts regardless of consequences or danger
- Arrogant; reveres heroes and conquests; tells braggadocious battle stories
- Might makes right; survive through might; a man's word is his vow.
- Strong leadership; Strict division of haves and have-nots.
- Exploits and manipulates; jealous, vengeful.

Cunning, without remorse, to get what they want. They seek revenge and expect to be avenged.

Example: The J writer tells the story of Cain and Abel, the sons of Adam and Eve, being jealous, resulting in murder, and avenge. They bring gifts to YHWH. YHWH is pleased with Abel's meat offering, but not as pleased with Cain's offering of the "fruit of the ground." Cain kills Abel out of jealousy. Then YHWH curses Cain and drives him away to spend his life wandering. The J writer says Cain will be avenged seven times. The theme of unforgiveness and vengefulness reoccurs, often using the number 7. Generations later, Lamech's sin will also be avenged seventy-times seven (Genesis 4, J writer).

Example: With the help of his mother Rachel, Jacob cheats Esau out of receiving their father Isaac's blessing. Mother and son are aware they could be cursed if Isaac doesn't fall for the trick. Rachel is willing to take the curse. After Jacob steals the blessing, Esau begs his father to bless him too, but Isaac follows the tribal code: only one blessing can be given out. The two brothers become estranged for decades. Later, it seems that Jacob gets his just rewards: he becomes the victim of a trick put upon him by his uncle Laban (Genesis 27-29, J writer).

Example: David's son Amnon covets and rapes his half-sister Tamar, David's daughter by a different wife. Then he despises her and is avenged by his brothers (2 Samuel 13, J writer).

Impulsive and Self-serving. King David was a warrior hero who took what he wanted. Representing the RED consciousness is a king with the emotional maturity of a teenager.

Example: King David enters a relationship with Bathsheba, the wife (property) of Uriah, David's army general. When Bathsheba becomes pregnant, David doesn't want Uriah to take revenge on him, so David has Uriah killed on the front lines of battle. David doesn't see anything wrong with that. Under tribal law, it was unacceptable to take the property or to kill someone from your tribe. Uriah was not of David's tribe, so it would have been acceptable for David to kill him. At this juncture in the story, the J writer demonstrated seeds of BLUE consciousness by introducing the prophet Nathan who tells David a story that causes a sense of remorse in the king (2 Samuel 11-12, J writer).

Arrogant. Reveres heroes and conquests. Tells braggadocious battle stories.

The book of Joshua reports story after story of warrior victories. Under YHWH's specific directions, Joshua's army utterly destroys villages, hangs kings, and enslaves entire tribes that try to trick them. We are told that all the surrounding kings were afraid. These stories about conquering Canaan vividly describe the chaos of the time, and true to the RED Warrior consciousness, they are biased toward the might of their people. (I came across a lecture about the Egyptian culture of that era. The speaker said, "In these stories, of course, the Egyptians are never harmed, and their enemies are utterly destroyed."[38] This is exactly what the Hebrews wrote about their enemies, the Egyptians.) Yet, there is little to no evidence that these mass killings occurred at that time.

Another example: In Genesis 34, the J writer tells of the rape of Dinah (a sister of the twelve sons of Jacob) and the brothers' revenge on the town of Shechem. It is a gruesome story that stuns modern readers. Richard Elliott Friedman posits that this and other violent stories of the conquest of Canaan do not correlate with any facts from history.[39]

Pre-morality and the status of women: Try to imagine a world without any awareness of BLUE's morality and sense of cooperation for the good of the community. That would be the world of our ancestors for thousands of years. Although people in the RED consciousness can understand social shame, they do not feel remorse for violating others' life and safety. The RED worldview is a masculine one: women were not considered equal to men, nor worthy of honor. The individualist male of the RED worldview would not be aware of nor capable of considering a woman's feelings or her dignity.

Example: When angels (male visitors) visited Abraham and his nephew Lot in Sodom, the men of Sodom wanted to engage in sexual activity with them. (When the J writer says, "to know them" it's a way of saying "to have sex with them.") Lot knows that refusing the crowd's demands would be dangerous, so he offers his virgin daughters instead, as he wants to honor his male guests. Lot's offer to turn over his virgin daughters was also not inappropriate as females were considered valuable property for trade and bargaining (Genesis 19, J writer).

Tribal loyalty to a vow. In the RED worldview, a vow is not to be broken, even if that means sacrificing something dear to you. Example: Jephthah of Gilead is described as one of the mighty warrior judges of early Israel. (He was an outcast because he was the son of a prostitute; an outlaw with a gang of followers, kicked out of his house by his 70 half-brothers. Judges 11: 1-3) When the Ammonites invaded Gilead, the elders of Gilead invited him to lead them to defend their territory. Jephthah said he would do it if they would make him their leader.) The night before he went into battle against the Ammonites, he wasn't so sure of the victory. He made a vow to YHWH: if YHWH would give him a victory over the Ammonites, Jephthah would make a burnt offering of whoever first came out of his doors when he returned victorious from the battle. "Then Jephthah came to his home at Mizpah, and there was his daughter coming out to meet him with timbrels and with dancing. She was his only child. . .. When he saw her, he tore his clothes, and said, 'Alas, my daughter! You have brought me very low; you have become the cause of great trouble to me. For I have opened my mouth to YHWH, and I cannot take back my vow.' So, she departed, she and her companions, and bewailed her virginity on the mountains. At the end of two months, she returned to her father, who did with her according to the vow he had made." (Judges 11: 29-39, J writer).

Perception of God through the RED Warrior, Egocentric Lens

The RED Warrior God

As the J writer tells her story of Joshua's and David's YHWH, she describes the kind of God of the predominantly RED "PowerGods" worldview. These Biblical heroes perceived a masculine PowerGod that must not be ignored. Rituals, ceremonies, and sacrifices to the warrior God were attempts to sway the God to support their battle, hunt, or invasion, and to celebrate the PowerGod after a battle.

From a predominantly RED consciousness, the warrior God is the force behind all victories. This God is displayed in the Bible as a masculine warrior, violent, spiteful, impulsive, persuadable, and uses male stand-ins to represent him.[9] "I hereby command you: Be strong and courageous; do not be frightened or dismayed, for the Lord your God is with you wherever you go.'" (Joshua 1: 9)

A violent, warrior god. From the perspective of those in the tribal warrior stage, "might makes right." There is no concept of diplomacy or talking things over. A strong fighter is what solves the problem. There are "600 passages of explicit violence in the Hebrew Bible, 1000 verses that describe God's violent actions in punishing humankind, 100 passages show God commanding his followers to kill people."[40] Acts of violence are not condemned, and no shame nor remorse is expected. In the following examples, notice the sense of heroism and the braggadocious tone of the stories.

Example: Five neighboring kings were afraid of YHWH's might, so they deceived Joshua's army so that they wouldn't have to meet them in battle. When Joshua found out, he took all their people as slaves. and hung the leaders. Then Joshua inspires the people: "'Do not be afraid or dismayed; be strong and courageous; for this YHWH will do to all the enemies against whom you fight.'(Joshua 1:9) Joshua took Makkedah on that day and struck it and its king with the edge of the sword; he utterly destroyed every person in it; he left no one remaining. And he did to the king of Makkedah as he had done to the king of Jericho" (Joshua 10:25-28, J writer). The same sentiment is repeated in Joshua 10:40; 1 Samuel 15 and several other references.

"He took all their kings, struck them down, and put them to death. Joshua made war a long time with all those kings. There was not a town that made peace with the Israelites, except the Hivites, the inhabitants of Gibeon; all were taken in battle." (Joshua 11:17b-19, J writer).

"The Lord is at your right hand; he will shatter kings on the day of this wrath. He will execute judgment among the nations, filling them with corpses; he will shatter heads over the wide earth." (Psalm

110: 5-6) (We can see all the vMemes represented in the Book of Psalms because it a collection of poems, prayers, and songs spanning 800 years, from the time of King David to the Second Temple period.)

An imminent, anthropomorphic god. In this stage, as in the previous one, God is very personal. He talks with his people and intervenes for them. Example: YHWH blesses Joshua, "I will be with you as I was with Moses. You are the one who shall command the priests who bear the ark of the covenant'. Joshua told the people that God is traveling with them. YHWH (which dwells in the ark of the covenant,) the Lord of all the earth is going to pass before you into the Jordan.' (Joshua 3: 7-11, J writer).

Another example of a personal, anthropomorphic perception of God: "YHWH regretted that he had made humankind on the earth. It grieved YHWH to his heart" (Genesis 6: 6, J writer).

A PowerGod is a being who unequivocally knows his existence and his unquestionable power. This is a healthy RED assertion. Example: When Moses meets God at the burning bush and asks God, "If I come to the Israelites and say to them, 'The God of your ancestors has sent me to you,' and they ask me, 'What is his name?' what shall I say to them?" God said to Moses, "I AM WHO I AM."[41] He said further, "Thus you shall say to the Israelites, 'I AM has sent me to you.'" (Exodus 3: 13-14, E writer).

A jealous god. Jealousy isn't very pretty, but it is a powerful motivator of the RED PowerGod. Example: The people perceived that YHWH had kept his covenant when he led them to victory against other tribes so they could have the land that he had promised to them. In return, YHWH demands their loyalty. This god commands that they do not intermarry, and they must remove other gods from their sight. (The pillars and Asherah in this passage refer to the altars of the female goddess in Canaan.) "Take care not to make a covenant with the inhabitants of the land to which you are going, or it will become a snare among you. You shall tear down their altars, break their pillars, and cut down their Asherahs. For you shall not bow to another god--because YHWH: His name is Jealous. He is a jealous God" (Exodus 34:12-14, the J writer's prologue to the earliest ten commandments).

This perception of a human-like God that is jealous, and demands sole loyalty indicates the RED and BLUE consciousness. For example: "The Israelites again did what was evil in the sight of the LORD, worshiping the Baals and the Astarte, the gods of Aram, the gods of Sidon, the gods of Moab, the gods of the Ammonites, and the gods of the Philistines. Thus, they abandoned the LORD and did not worship him. So, the anger of the LORD was kindled against Israel, and he sold them into the hand of the Philistines and into the hand of the Ammonites." (Judges 10:6-7 P writer) See also see 1 Kings 11:33, D writer and Numbers 14:8-9, P writer.

A spiteful god. Spite is a common idea in a predominant RED consciousness. If you believe that your god is spiteful, you could accept the idea that it is this god that caused your suffering. Example: The early writers convey the belief that the Great Flood was an act of a god who has a spiteful reaction to the troubles going on with human society (Genesis 5, J writer).

Example: The Tower of Babel conveys a God who is jealous, spiteful, and afraid of losing his powerful leverage. "YHWH said, 'Look, they are one people, and they have all one language; and this is only the beginning of what they will do; nothing that they propose to do will now be impossible for them. Come, let us go down, and confuse their language there so that they will not understand one another's speech.' So, YHWH scattered them abroad from there over the face of all the earth, and they left off building the city" (Genesis 11, J writer).

Example: "For it was YHWH's doing to harden their hearts so that they would come against Israel in battle, in order that they might be utterly destroyed, and might receive no mercy, but be exterminated, just as YHWH had commanded Moses" (Joshua 11:20, J writer).

Another example of a spiteful god: The destruction of Sodom
and Gomorrah depicts YHWH as the cause of the raining fire and
brimstone that destroys everyone. When Lot's wife turns around to
see the burning village, God turns her into a pillar of salt. (Genesis
19, J writer). We can see why the ancient prayers regularly asked
YHWH for mercy.

An impulsive, persuadable god. The gods of the ancient myths
seemed more human than divine. They would make deals with
humans, and they would get angry and jealous, and dish out swift
punishment. This is a projection of the RED stage of consciousness.
Example: After YHWH threatens to destroy Sodom and Gomorrah,
Abraham boldly cajoles YHWH to back off on his threat. "Then
Abraham came near and said, 'Will you indeed sweep away the
righteous with the wicked? Suppose there are fifty righteous within
the city; will you then sweep away the place and not forgive it for the
fifty righteous who are in it? Far be it from you to do such a thing, to
slay the righteous with the wicked, so that the righteous fare as the
wicked! Far be that from you! Shall not the Judge of all the earth do
what is just?' And YHWH said, 'If I find at Sodom fifty righteous
in the city, I will forgive the whole place for their sake'" (Genesis
18:23-26, J writer). Abraham continues to bargain until YHWH
agrees to spare the city if just ten righteous people are found there.
In the end, however, after Lot's botched encounter with YHWH's
angels, YHWH did destroy the entire city, allowing only Lot and
his wife and children to escape.

Another example: While Moses was up on Mount Sinai with
YHWH, receiving the commandments, the people convinced Moses'
brother Aaron to build an image of a golden calf, the symbol of the
local Baal. YHWH had threatened to annihilate them all, but Moses
persuaded YHWH to back down. "And YHWH relented about the
bad he had spoken to do to His people." (Exodus 32:14, E writer).

Read David's prayer for pardon in Psalm 51. "Have mercy on me,
O God, according to your steadfast love; according to your abundant
mercy blot out my transgressions. Wash me thoroughly from my

iniquity and cleanse me from my sin. ... Create in me a clean heart, O God, and put a new and right spirit within me. Do not cast me away from your presence, and do not take your holy spirit from me." (Psalm 51: 1-2, 10-11) We can see the perception of God in David's mind: God is very human-like and egocentric: unreliable, vengeful, and persuadable. God might just reject David because of his sin.

A male god who uses male stand-ins. In the stories when angels or strangers appear, if pronouns are used, they are masculine. There is no appearance of a female angel recorded in the Hebrew Bible. Example: "And he said, 'Hear my words: When there are prophets among you, I, YHWH make myself known to them in visions; I speak to them in dreams. Not so with my servant Moses. He is entrusted with all my house. With him I speak face to face—clearly, not in riddles; and he beholds the form of the Lord'" (Numbers 12:6-8, E writer).

Revisiting Three Prevalent Biblical Discrepancies

In this section and a corresponding section in Chapter 6, we will revisit the three discrepancies posited in Chapter 2, "Authorship Explains Three Prevalent Biblical Discrepancies."

Writer J's Creation Myth

Read the creation story in Genesis 2-3 to get a glimpse of the J writer's purple/RED[42] worldview. The J writer describes a PURPLE magical view and a RED impulsive, illogical creation process. The creator is intensely immanent, personable, and spontaneous. J employs a talking snake and explains that YHWH breathed into a lump of clay to create the human body. YHWH walks and talks with the humans, and the woman was able to hide from God." In the story of the temptation of Eve in the Garden of Eden, the J writer illustrates polytheism: a jealous YHWH fears that the humans might "become like one of us, to know good and bad." (Genesis 3:22) This view of a plural god-consciousness is also recorded by the J writer in the Tower of Babel story in Genesis 11.

Writer J's Great Flood Myth

Genesis 6: 5-8, Genesis 7: 1-5, 7, 10, 12, 16b-20, 22-23, Genesis 8: 2b-3a, 6, 8-12, 13b, 20-22

Around 7500 BCE there was a great flood related to the ice melt that marked the end of the Ice Age and the beginning of agricultural technology. Mesopotamia's Saga of Gilgamesh (c. 1800 BCE) incorporates a great flood, as does other cultural mythology. Unique to the Hebrew story is the perception that it was YHWH's disappointment with humans that caused the great flood.

J creates a story that describes an interpersonal immanent god. This god regretted creating humans because they had turned out so evil. (Genesis 6: 6) This god made sure Noah's family was safely on board, then closed the doors of the ark himself. (Genesis 6: 16b) In J's worldview, animal sacrifice to the gods was expected, which is why J wrote that YHWH told them to take seven pairs of all the pure animals. (Genesis 7: 2) They are the animals that are fit to be used as a sacrifice. When this very immanent god smelled the odor of the meat being sacrificed, he was pleased. (Genesis 8: 21 J writer).

The J writer's myths are not unique to the Hebrew people. They have a similar tone to myths from neighboring cultures, especially Babylon.

Writer J's Ten Commandments, Tenth Century BCE

Exodus 34:10-26

The J writer recorded ten laws that address the values and practices of nomadic tribes of the twelve sons of Jacob. They reflect the Purple/RED vMeme. YHWH is a braggadocious RED PowerGod who demands loyalty. "I'm making a covenant. Before all your people, I'll do wonders that haven't been created in all the earth, and among all the nations and all the people whom you're among will see YHWH's deeds because that which I'm doing with you is awesome." (Exodus 34: 10)[43] In exchange, he demands that they not mix with others that are in the land he promises to deliver. These Purple/RED pre-axial age commandments are a window into the governing values of the time. They are tribal codes of conduct that dictate honoring their god with tithes, festivals, and rituals. Rules like 'don't eat their food, don't marry their women' display the PURPLE distrust of others, and instructions on the treatment of food address the BEIGE survival techniques necessary for nomadic living. They do not focus on any ethical and moral behavior in society since those values have not yet emerged. Here is a summary of the J writer's ten commandments: (Exodus 34:10-26)

1. Worship no other god.
2. Make no covenant with aliens. (Tear down their altars, pillars, and sacred poles. If you mix with them, you'll end up intermarrying and eating unclean food. This will corrupt your people.
3. Do not make molten (metal cast) idols.
4. Keep the Festival of Unleavened Bread. (Eat unleavened bread for 7 days in the month of Abib, the month of the exodus from Egypt.)
5. Bring the firstborn from the womb to YHWH. (specifically, ox, and sheep. Use a sheep to redeem (replace the sacrifice of) your first-born son.
6. Work six days, rest on the seventh day.
7. Observe three Festivals: Weeks, the wheat harvest, and the Gathering. Three times per year, all the men must "appear before the Lord YHWH, God of Israel."
8. Don't offer sacrificial blood with leavened bread. Don't leave any of the Passover sacrifices until morning.
9. Bring the first harvest to the house of YHWH.
10. Don't boil a kid goat in its mother's milk.

Seeds of Consciousness

As mentioned in Chapter 4, sometimes we come across isolated "seeds" of consciousness: ideas that are before their time. In the period of the Judges and the early kingdom, the story of the early prophet Nathan plants a seed of the future Post-Modern values.

Example: The Relationship Between Saul and David: 1 Samuel 16, 21, 22, 23, 24, 26, and 31

The J writer tells the story of Samuel who was raised by the priest/judge Eli and was called to the priesthood by a divine calling. When Samuel was old, the people demanded that he appoint a king. Despite Samuel's repeated warning to the people about wanting a king rather than recognizing YHWH as their king, he anointed Saul from the tribe of Benjamin as their first king. But Saul's reign lasted only two years. He performed an unlawful sacrifice, declared a rash oath, and lost his political influence. "YHWH said to Samuel, 'I regret that I made Saul king, for he has turned his back on me'" (1 Samuel 15:11, J writer). YHWH directed Samuel to secretly anoint the young boy David to be the next king. While waiting to become king, David served Saul as armor-bearer and music therapist. On the battlefield, David proves himself worthy to be a warrior-king by killing the Philistine named Goliath. In time, it becomes obvious that the people favor David over Saul, and Saul becomes extremely jealous. Saul makes numerous attempts to take David's life but David escapes and hides. And here is the seed of consciousness: David is kind and respectful to Saul, his mentor and elder. He consistently refuses to kill Saul, saying, "YHWH forbid that I should raise my hand against him for he is YHWH's anointed." By putting these words into the mouth of David, the J writer shows a seed of BLUE consciousness: a glimpse of respect for order and an acknowledgment of an authoritarian god.

Another example: As mentioned earlier in this chapter, King David adds Bathsheba into his ever-expanding collection of women, and the prophet Nathan confronts him and introduces the emerging BLUE morality. Nathan tells David a story about a rich man who takes away the one little ewe lamb of his poor neighbor. Using this parable, Nathan helps David realize his deceptions were shameful. The J writer, through Nathan's voice, introduces a seed of the BLUE consciousness: a call to a higher moral code. Read 2nd Samuel 11-12

An Invitation to Stretch into Integral Consciousness

Today's reader might be appalled at the acceptance of violence in the J and E writer's stories. Why would the people of that time be so willing to follow utterly unconscionable superstitions and agreements? Why would they record rapes and slaughters? These questions are compounded by the probability that these events did not occur. Scholars have found no archeological proof that this land had been conquered by the Israelites. There are no ruins or mass burial grounds to substantiate such devastating conquests. Then why would they boast of such violence and why would they record such horrible stories? Why wouldn't they be ashamed of them?

Upon reading Judges 11, we might ask why Jephthah didn't break his vow to preserve the life of his daughter. Why didn't Jephthah's daughter rebel against her father's vow? Be sure to read the first few verses of this chapter to get a sense of what vMeme Jephthah would have considered to be his predominant vMeme.

Working with the Spiral, we are invited to approach each vMeme from an integral perspective. What were J and E's worldviews in 1000 BCE? Try to imagine living in a world that has not yet conceived of the BLUE vMeme code of conduct and morality, where there is no awareness of ideas like "Thou shalt not kill." The norm for thousands of years was to take what you want by force. They were unaware that violence was not the only way to get what a person wants.

In that world of purple/RED consciousness (with no BLUE morals), post-battle fictional bragging and boasting were acceptable, expected, and even entertaining. Additionally, before the introduction of BLUE values, a woman was not valued as a human being. Like the livestock, a woman was a man's property, and there was no consideration of her rights or her honor. Further, human sacrifice was prominent in Purple and early RED. Under RED loyalty codes, a man's vow was more important than the rights or the honor of a woman, more important than any thought of mercy. Mercy and forgiveness would not play into thought until BLUE consciousness emerged.

It is a worldview quite different from a contemporary perspective. We are invited to withhold from imposing our views about women, violence, and humanity on this earlier worldview. This is an invitation to release our judgment towards those who operate from a RED worldview and recognize it as a predictable stage in the development of consciousness. Contemporary judgment is driven by our values of BLUE, ORANGE, and GREEN. We have a hard time imagining why anyone would be proud of such violence. But from a Purple/RED perspective, far from ORANGE's reasoning abilities and GREEN's compassion, we can value such stories.

Read J's account of what happened in Noah's family immediately following the great flood (Genesis 9:18-27). The J writer uses this story to explain why the Canaanites are enemies of the Hebrew people, but her story also unwittingly indicates an evolutionary leap from hunter-gatherer to agriculture. Many readers have wondered why the writer notes that Noah planted a vineyard as soon as the flood water receded and got drunk on the wine. Readers become very uncomfortable to learn that his daughters chose to lay with him. Keep in mind that this story was written by the J writer who did not have the BLUE moral values of today's world, which today's readers assume everyone knows. J's story illustrates a culturally immature writer who has revealed in the straightforward storytelling style, the personal, human-like YHWH, and the "warts and all" of the biblical characters.

The J and E writers wrote the stories from a RED consciousness that knew nothing of BLUE's values of morality. Since they were literate, we can assume they were educated, would they not have had some sense of the rising BLUE morality at that time? Yet these writers did not try to soften the violent amoral behavior of the characters. Perhaps their intention for recording these stories was to provide the setting for the awakening BLUE worldview. Whatever J and E's intentions, they have given us a window into the pre-moral consciousness.

For those of us who were taught Jewish or Christian religion, we can free ourselves from the turmoil we've felt about these ancient stories by applying the lens of Spiral Dynamics. Probably, we will find that many of our questions are answered when we view the characters' actions and decisions through the consciousness of their vMeme.

The Bible books considered in this study of RED in the Bible are most of Genesis and Exodus, parts of Numbers, most of Joshua and Judges, most of 1 and 2 Samuel, and parts of the first two chapters of 1 Kings.[44]

Don't Skip This Section! Interesting thoughts, anecdotes, and prompts for discussion.

(numbers are for reference only and do not indicate a suggested order or importance.)

1. Genesis 12 tells us that Abraham came out of Ur and brought his people into the area around the Jordan. What "people" did Abraham represent and why did he leave Ur? Watch this video from Epimetheus who offers a fascinating explanation without directly mentioning Abraham and the Israelites. *What was Life Like After the Bronze Age Collapse?* https://youtu. be/U5RCjvKVL38. Epimetheus explains that nomadic tribes had always lived on the outskirts of the society of the Fertile Crescent. When the Bronze Age infrastructure fell apart, toppling the elite and the merchants, farms, and markets, the nomadic tribes who had survived with their herds in the tough arid countryside, moved into and thrived in the places that had fallen. Epimetheus' explanation provides a

reasonable explanation of how Abraham's generations could have moved into Canaan.

2. Learn more: Watch *History of Ancient Israel and Judah Explained in 5 Minutes*. This YouTube video contains a brief explanation of the political events in Hebrew history from the Judges to the Kingdoms to the Roman period. Produced by Epimetheus, April 9, 2018. 5:39 minutes <u>History of Ancient Israel and Judah in 5 minutes. https://youtu.be/ZybFYikBMLg</u>

3. Apply: In the section "Revisiting the Creation Myth," we noted that the writer portrays God as petty and impulsive, which suggests that the writer operates in the RED consciousness. Explore this further in a discussion group or through personal contemplation. Discussion Prompt: We imagine God at our point of consciousness: we create an imaginary picture of God from our predominant worldview. Consider this observation and share examples in your experience to back up or refute this observation.

4. The period of the judges is covered by the J writer with lively stories about three judges: Abimelech, born of a concubine in Shechem, (Judges 8: 29- 57) The story of Jephthah (Judges 10: 8 – 11: 40.), and the story of Sampson (Judges 13: 2 – 16: 31). A few of those verses are from the later writer who felt compelled to tack locations and other details. When you read these stories, you'll see the RED characteristics of the J writer's consciousness. Compare these stories to the long story about Gideon recorded in Judges 6: 11-8: 28, written by someone long after the era. Do you see a marked difference in emphasis? What is it?

5. Consider how you relate to this paradigm constructed by the RED/blue perception of God. Reread the section "A Jealous God." The perception that God is a jealous god, demanding sole loyalty, develops further in the BLUE worldview. This premise infers setting oneself aside from all other groups that don't adhere to your religious practice, is the foundation of all traditional religions. Consider the phrase, "There is only one

God, and that's *our* God!" That very BLUE statement could come from a fundamentalist Jew, a Moslem, or a Christian. Each of these religions comes from the God of Abraham, yet all are consistent with all levels in the First Tier of the Spiral because each thinks theirs is the only right way to follow this God.

6. What about the Exodus? The Biblical story of the exodus from Egypt is absent historical points of reference. There is no archeological nor historical proof that 600,000 men exited Egypt at any given time (Exodus 12: 37, E writer). If 600,000 men left, their women and children would have gone with them. This mass migration would have included upwards of two million people! It's more likely that the exodus involved a much smaller number of people, perhaps only the Levites. Interested in learning more? Read Richard Elliott Friedman's *The Exodus*. Also, refer to Israel Finkelstein's *The Bible Unearthed* Chapter 2 *Did the Exodus Happen?*[45]

7. Contemplate the worldview of the J writer. Read Genesis 19. The destruction of Sodom and Gomorrah shows YHWH as the cause of the fire and brimstone and the cause of Lot's wife turning into a pillar of salt. Brimstone is the biblical name for sulfur, which typically comes from volcanos or hot springs. Consider that this biblical story may have been a Purple/RED myth to help the people make sense of the climate crisis that took place at the end of the Bronze Age. The perception that God punishes through natural phenomena is still alive in our collective consciousness, especially since BLUE religion turned the biblical myth into the infallible word of God, and therefore declared it "fact." Similarly, the "conquest of Canaan" is told as if God had made the other tribes crumble. The Bronze Age collapsed due to various contributing factors which weren't apparent at the time, so the people could have attributed the drastic change in "life conditions"[46] to God's intervention. In retrospect, we can see that these major changes in life conditions were a catalyst for a

new value system to arise. As with all major shifts, there are a variety of factors that contribute to birthing a new paradigm. Through our integral lens, we can see that our ancestors who had no awareness of science and no reasoning abilities, would attribute these factors to God's intervention.

8. Reflect: "Living constantly poised against attack, and ready for war, the beleaguered people developed an embattled cult."[47] Karen Armstrong's comment reveals a paradox within RED consciousness that is easily overlooked: *aggression* is linked with the *victim*. When the predominant consciousness is "warrior," there will be a strong victim consciousness within the population. The warrior's greatest fear is that they will become victims, and as they conquer, they leave a trail of victims. Egocentric RED brags about its power, regardless of how it might have hurt others. Simultaneously, when the egocentric RED experiences a setback, it whines and groans like a victim because it didn't get what it wanted. Where you find RED egocentricity you can assume the presence of victim-consciousness. Reflect on how RED has made its appearance in your life, and how that includes both sides of this paradox.

9. Self-Awareness: The section, "An Invitation to Stretch into Integral Consciousness" states, "Under RED loyalty codes, a man's vow was more important than the rights or the honor of a woman." If you are ready to look at the shadows in your life or the collective consciousness, consider the woman's place in a RED paradigm of your own culture. It can be found, for example, in domestic violence cycles. If you have been in a relationship like that, consider its RED characteristics. Consider your place as a woman or as a man in that cultural paradigm.

10. David is a paradox: Read the story of David in 1 and 2 Samuel and the beginning of 1 Kings. In what ways is David himself a paradoxical character? What kind of figure is he? What do you make of him, both as a man and as a king?

Chapter 6:

An Authoritarian God: BLUE vMeme in the Bible

"He has told you, O mortal, what is good; and what does YHWH require of you but to do justice, and to love kindness, and to walk humbly with your God?" (Micah 6:6-8).

The era from the eighth to the third centuries BCE is dubbed the Axial Age,[48] a pivotal time in humankind's consciousness. It was a time when similar religious and philosophical constructs appeared around the globe without any direct cultural contact between those peoples. Spiritual teachers around the globe (Zoroaster, the Buddha, Confucius, Lao Tzu, and the Hebrew prophets) expressed new values and practices to live fruitfully and meaningfully. In the Middle East region, the Axial Age marks the emergence of the Spiral Dynamics BLUE vMeme. From this new worldview arose a moral code with an emphasis on law and order, hierarchy and status, duty, and self-sacrifice.

Historical Context to the era that produced the majority of the Hebrew Bible

In 922 BCE, the Israelite kingdom was divided. Ten tribes in the north centralized in Samaria and called themselves Israel. Two tribes in the south were centralized in Jerusalem and called themselves Judah. The next century saw relative calm. The wealthy House of Omri, with the infamous King Ahab and his queen Jezebel, (876-842) were prosperous as they traded with other surrounding nations and tolerated their polytheism. This was perceived as evil by the southern priests who insisted on devoted monotheism and exclusivity. The prophet Elijah tried to get Ahab to turn away from the idols. Stories of this Divided Kingdom period appear in the books of 1 and 2 Kings. (The Deuteronomistic writers wrote 1 and 2 Kings in the fifth century.)

Eighth Century BCE

The prophet Amos introduced challenging ethical standards for the community during Israel's stable forty-year period under King Jeroboam II. But then, as mentioned in Chapter 2, Assyria moved forcefully into the region. Israel succumbed to Assyria's onslaughts in 722 BCE. The prophets Amos and Hosea speak of this period of significant change in life conditions for the people of Israel and Judah. The federation of twelve tribes, the sons of Jacob, no longer existed. Some refugees assimilated into Judah, while others fled to many corners of the known world.

Judah survived Assyria's invasion by agreeing to pay an annual tax to Assyria. King Hezekiah (715-687) took the throne shortly after Israel fell, and instituted religious reform, taking down all the poles and symbols that referred to the other gods. Knowing that this small, isolated territory of Judah was vulnerable to further attack, Hezekiah built an underground tunnel to supply water to Jerusalem.

The P writer was active in Judah at this time, documenting rituals, laws, and punishments, adding locations, ancestry, and names into the JE writings, and honoring Hezekiah's reign.[49] The Redactor of the J and E writings (RJE) also worked during the reign of Hezekiah. Micah and "First Isaiah" (Isaiah 1-39) address the issues in Judah immediately following the fall of Israel.

Seventh Century BCE

While a vassal of Assyria, Judah had a prosperous century. Hezekiah had enforced a strict mandate for the sole worship of YHWH. His successors, however, forgot the ways of YHWH and returned to polytheism. Then King Josiah came to the throne (640-609) and introduced substantial religious reform and a centralized theocracy. Toward the end of the century, the once flourishing capital of the Assyrian Empire, Nineveh (the city that Jonah is said to have visited), was destroyed by Babylon, the next rising empire. Writings from this century include the book of Deuteronomy (Dtr[1]), Nahum, Habakkuk, Zechariah, Zephaniah, and Jeremiah.

Sixth Century BCE

After Babylon defeated Assyria, Judah refused to pay tribute to the new regime, so the Babylonian army began a siege of Judah. The elites were exiled to Babylon around 598 BCE. By 586 BCE, after pillaging the resources and trampling the land of Judah, the army broke through Jerusalem's walls and burned the temple. The Tabernacle (the tent that sheltered the Ark of the Covenant) was lost in the fire. Many of the people were exiled to Babylon. Others fled to Egypt, and others remained in the burned-out countryside of Judah.

With Jerusalem and the beloved Temple destroyed, the Hebrew peoples' religious, cultural, and spiritual home was lost. The poor were left to survive in the ruined city and countryside, and the "song of Zion" was muted. The literature of the Exile includes Psalm 137, the book of Lamentations, and the last part of the book of Jeremiah, reflecting the refugees' life in Egypt. We can also read of this era of captivity in the entire book of Ezekiel, and the book of Isaiah chapters 40-55, reflecting the exiles' life in Babylonia. "It is not happy literature. Some of it expresses bitterness. Much of it expresses guilt. (Why did this happen to us? It must be that *we* did something wrong.) Just about all of it expresses sadness."[50] The exile ended after roughly two generations. Persia conquered Babylon in 538 BCE and Persia's King Cyrus sent the Judeans back to Judah to rebuild. In addition to Jeremiah and Second Isaiah, other sixth-century prophets and writers were Joel, Obadiah, Haggai, Zechariah, Daniel, and Dtr^2.

Fifth Century BCE
Gradually the exiles returned to their territory and began rebuilding the city of Jerusalem and the Temple, marking the beginning of the Second Temple Period. This reconstruction project was led by Ezra and Nehemiah. Their new territory, much smaller than before, is now a Persian province called Yehud. Fifth-century prophets were: "Third Isaiah" (Isaiah 56-66), Malachi, Ezra, Nehemiah, and Dtr^3.

The Deuteronomistic School: Centuries of Hebrew Theological Development

During this momentous period surrounding the destruction of Jerusalem, many scribes, known as the "Deuteronomistic School," produced great quantities of written work, the contents of which eventually became a large portion of the Hebrew canon. There are three different phases of the D writings:

1. Dtr[1] wrote under King Josiah. (640-609 BCE)
2. Dtr[2] wrote in response to the destruction of Jerusalem, the deportations, and the exile. (circa 605-538)
3. Dtr[3] wrote after the exiles returned to Jerusalem, circa 520s BCE, the beginning of "the Second Temple Period."

"Dtr[1]," who wrote during King Josiah's Golden Age, considered Josiah's reign the height of the story of their people, the culmination of YHWH's covenant with the House of David. These writings expound on Moses' farewell and retell the "Deuteronomistic History" that weaves in the immorality of worshipping other gods and the effects of disobeying the covenant with YHWH. This was the lesson they had learned from seeing Israel fall to Assyria. Dtr[1] is the voice of the religious reform of King Josiah. This writer produced a "hidden" scroll that contained a second telling, a revised version, of the stories of previous generations with a new underlying message of God and the covenant, reform, and repentance. This second telling of the Hebrew myth became known as the book of Deuteronomy, ("deutero" means second), and it became the primary narrative of the Hebrew people during the period before the destruction of the Temple. The first half of Deuteronomy (chapters 1-11) is a revised story of the end of Moses' life, with a big parting speech from Moses and his gift of the scroll (the one that was produced by Dtr[1].) The second half of Deuteronomy (chapters 12-26) explains the Law Code, which included a requirement of centralized worship in Jerusalem, a law that the King must be chosen by YHWH, and cannot be a foreigner, the Ten Commandments, and other laws about charity and justice, and dietary laws, etc. The scroll was read publicly every day, teaching the people about their God. In the retelling of the story, the theological cycle of covenant, sin, and repentance is woven throughout. When Israel fell and Judah became a vassal of a huge empire, the people developed a new way of seeing their covenant with God. This pivotal change displays all the characteristics of the BLUE Authoritarian, Absolutist vMeme of Spiral Dynamics.

The Dtr[2] writers are the prophet Jeremiah and his scribe Baruch Ben Neriah. During the Babylonian exile, they wrote the entire books of Jeremiah and Lamentations and parts of Deuteronomy. These writings provide a moral reason why Judah was destroyed: the people disobeyed YHWH and they had to be punished. "And a later generation will say . . . when they'll see that the land's plagues and its illnesses that YHWH put in it, brimstone, and salt, all the land a 'burning, it won't be seeded and won't grow, . . . and all the nations will say, 'For what did YHWH do something like this to this land? What is this big flaring of anger?'" (Deuteronomy 29:21-23, Dtr2).[51]

The Dtr[3] writers wrote during the early Second Temple Period (post 500 BCE). These writers also inserted a theological theme: a recurring cycle of infidelity, punishment, repentance, and forgiveness.

These later writers set the tone for a new Hebrew way of living. It would be characterized by obedience, devotion to YHWH and the law and practices, cooperation, and mutual respect. And they provided an explanation for God's anger, bringing to light the idea that your actions have consequences. The people had begun to believe in a god of justice and mercy. This is indicative of the BLUE worldview.

Perception of the World Through the BLUE Lens in the Hebrew Scriptures

The authoritarian absolutist consciousness creates the idea of monotheism: there is only one true God and there is only one true religion. All other gods and religions are false and must be removed from one's consciousness. Loyalty to their God, religion, culture, values, and language is essential. All world religions emerged out of the Axial Age (or BLUE vMeme). We can see this value system in all brands of fundamentalist religion and hierarchical social systems, like caste systems, racism, and nationalism. Many healthy aspects of BLUE must be included in every society: a healthy respect for the law, careful attention to detail and precision, healthy authority, and hierarchy, and cooperation with standards of conduct.

The BLUE vMeme is a response to the self-indulgent worldview of the past. It is a "we" mindset that values community over individuality, emphasizing self-sacrifice for the good of the whole. In the Authoritarian mindset, order, discipline, meaning, and purpose are the new values. Absolute rules (from God) are established. This worldview's myths of feature heroes who follow those rules and humbly obey their God. The myths offer reminders that disobeying these rules brings horrible consequences. These stories called the people to repent and conform for the greater good. (See the Appendix for more on the BLUE vMeme.)

The bulk of the Hebrew Bible was written during the emerging BLUE paradigm by the Priestly and Deuteronomistic (P and D) writers and the biblical prophets. This literature was a fresh look at a new world. The early writers' heroic stories of violence and self-indulgence (the fading RED worldview) were vehemently rejected by these writers and replaced by mythic morality stories of self-sacrifice and discipline, humility, and service to God and each other. These written words became understood as the direct revelation of an absolute and singular God.

Values of the BLUE TruthForce[52] vMeme that are expressed by the Axial Age Biblical writers.

- "We" collective identity, "we vs. they"
- Authoritarian: Hierarchical, Values Obedience, Loyalty

- Monotheism Devotion to the One God
- Right Living; purposeful living.
- Absolute truth.
- Attention to Detail and Precision.
- Nationalistic; the worldview is larger than the tribe or ethnic group.

Authoritarian: Hierarchy, Monotheism. This vMeme believes that humankind is accountable to a higher authority. It values obedience, loyalty, and attentive devotion to the One God. Obey the laws and rituals, and morality codes. Deny your desires for the sake of a higher cause. If you do your part in society and if you are righteous "in God's eyes," you will experience order, security, and stability. It's a matter of duty, responsibility, self-discipline, and humility. Awareness of remorse and guilt; accepts penalties for disobedience; morality, suffering, and sacrifice.

Values Right Living. purposeful living, self-discipline, and devotion Following the norms is a responsibility, and duty, motivated by religion, patriotism, cooperation, and guilt.

God requires blameless leaders. **"**Noah was a virtuous man. He was unblemished in his generations. Noah walked with God. . .. According to everything that God commanded him, he did so" (Genesis 6:9 and 6:22, P writer).

"YHWH appeared to Abram and said to him, walk before me and be unblemished, and let me place my covenant between me and you." (Genesis 17:1b-2, P writer).

Absolute truth. An ultimate truth dictates personal and societal order, purpose, and direction. This vMeme has a developmental stage that operates at a Concrete-literal level of thinking, similar to an unquestioning, complicit adult or child. The laws are explicit and must be followed precisely. There is absolute right and wrong: no "grey area" in this worldview. Likewise, order; justice, and mercy are not up for interpretation.

Example: Notice that the writer deems it necessary to elaborate exactly on what it means to be righteous. "If a man is righteous and does what is lawful and right—if he does not eat upon the mountains or lift up his eyes to the idols of the house of Israel, does not defile his neighbor's wife or approach a woman during her menstrual period, does not oppress anyone, but restores to the debtor his pledge, commits no robbery, gives his bread to the hungry and covers the naked with a garment, does not take advance or accrued interest, withholds his hand from iniquity, executes true justice between contending parties, follows my statutes, and is careful to observe my ordinances, acting faithfully—such a one is righteous; he shall surely live, says the LORD GOD." (Ezekiel 18: 5-9. Written during the Babylonian Exile).

Attention to Order and Precision. The Authoritarian worldview introduces disciplined attention to detail and precision.

The writing style of the P and D writers indicates a command of language and the written word that isn't apparent in the earlier writers. This is indicative of the rising BLUE consciousness. The BLUE worldview values order, organization, detailed record keeping, and precise language. The BLUE writer is concerned with accuracy: he records people's ages, times when an event took place and how long it took, etc. The P writer was a documenter, a record keeper, and an instruction-giver.

"And the ark rested in the seventh month, in the seventeenth day of the month, on the mountains of Ararat. And the water went on receding until the tenth month. In the tenth month, in the first day of the month, the mountains appeared" (Genesis 8, P writer).

"These are the families of Noah's (Shem, Ham, and Japheth) children by their records in their nations" (Genesis 10:32, P writer).

"Bury me in the cave that is in the field of Ephron, the Hittite, in the cave that's in the field of Machpelah, which faces Mamre in the land of Canaan" (Genesis 49:29-30, P writer).

"And some of the people of Judah, Benjamin, Ephraim, and Manasseh lived in Jerusalem: Uthai son of Anmihud, son of Omri, son of Imri, son of Bani, from the sons of Perez son of Judah" (1 Chronicles 9:3 P writer).

In addition to the attention to detail, notice the BLUE perception of God as the authority: YHWH spoke to Moses saying, "Speak to the children of Israel that they shall take a donation for me...gold and silver and bronze . . . and blue and purple and scarlet . . . oil and spices and . . . stones . . . And they shall make an ark of acacia wood, its length two and a half cubits and its width a cubit and a half. And you shall plate it with pure gold . . . and you shall cast four rings of gold for it and place them on four bases . . . and you shall make poles and bring the poles through the rings. And you shall make the Tabernacle with ten curtains of woven linen and blue and purple and scarlet, with cherubs, you shall make them designer's work" (Exodus 25-26, selected P writings).

Nationalistic; the worldview is larger than the tribe or ethnic group. In previous stages of development, the circle of community is very small: family and tribe. In this stage, the territory expands. Joshua 15 contains a lengthy description of all the land that the tribes conquered, including details of locations and landmarks. Judah's land area extended south to the "boundary of Edom, to the wilderness of Zin at the farthest south. And their southern boundary ran from the end of the Dead Sea from the bay that faces southwards" (Joshua 15:1-3, D writer). This was the work of the D writer, who had seen how the tribes were distributed and wanted to get it all on record. He was establishing the legacy of the Israelites as a sovereign nation, with an eye on other powers gaining strength in the region.

Perception of God through the BLUE Authoritarian, Absolutist Lens

The BLUE vMeme introduces monotheism focused on a singular masculine God who expects devotion, discipline, service, and self-sacrifice and rewards faithfulness and dedication. This God is the ultimate authority: loves justice and provides laws and codes of conduct, purity, and devotion. He is an authoritarian, anthropomorphic, almighty father figure. He makes agreements to take care of his people but expects devotion in return for his providence. He is loving but vengeful, anthropomorphized but not personal. He is transcendent, but he will answer prayer if the prayer is sincere. He gives comfort and favors his own. He is patriarchal, has a very masculine demeanor, and uses male stand-ins. This God of the BLUE vMeme is absolute, meaning he is unchanging and unchangeable. Unlike the RED God, He cannot be cajoled. His laws do not change, and he is timeless.

The BLUE Authoritarian God

A singular God Who expects Obedience, Loyalty, and Attentive Devotion. The Jewish daily prayer known as *the Shema* which means 'to hear,' consists of three passages in the Hebrew Bible.[53] These passages, written by the P and D writers, call the people to "hear" or pay attention to and be disciplined about these teachings. *The Shema* is a wonderful illustration of some core values of the BLUE vMeme: obey, and venerate the one ultimate, absolute Authority. If you do, you will be rewarded. Be devoted: don't be distracted by this world.

The first of these passages addresses loving devotion to the One God, with clear directives about practicing this teaching. "Hear, O Israel: The LORD is our God, the LORD alone. You shall love the LORD your God with all your heart, and with all your soul, and with all your might. Keep these words that I am commanding you today in your heart. Recite them to your children and talk about them when you are at home and when you are away, when you lie down and when you rise. Bind them as a sign on your hand, fix them as an emblem on your forehead, and write them on the doorposts of your house and on your gates." (Deuteronomy 6: 4-9. Dtr¹)

In the second passage of *the Shema*, the people learn to value loyalty, service, and obedience to God, and hear that it will be rewarded with future prosperity. "If you will only heed his every commandment that I am commanding you today—loving the LORD your God, and serving him with all your heart and with all your soul— then he will give the rain for your land in its season, the early rain and the later rain, and you will gather in your grain, your wine, and your oil; and he will give grass in your fields for your livestock, and you will eat your fill. Take care, or you will be seduced into turning away, serving other gods, and worshiping them. (Deuteronomy 11: 13-16. Dtr[1])

The third passage of *the Shema* commands a distinctive practice of devotion and discipline. "The LORD said to Moses: 'Speak to the Israelites and tell them to make fringes on the corners of their garments throughout their generations and to put a blue cord on the fringe at each corner. You have the fringe so that when you see it, you will remember all the commandments of the LORD and do them, and not follow the lust of your own heart and your own eyes. So you shall remember and do all my commandments, and you shall be holy to your God. I am the LORD your God, who brought you out of the land of Egypt, to be your God: I am the LORD your God." (Numbers 15: 37-41. P writer)

A God Who rewards Devotion: The story of the Hebrew nation as retold by the P and D writers, has a pattern of obedience, defiance, remorse, and a return to obedience. It is an epic story and the dominant theme of the Jewish faith. Through these stories, the Torah introduces a relationship between YHWH and the people When Jacob was chosen by YHWH, he got a new name and an entirely new identity. He was to be completely devoted to God. "God appeared to Jacob, and he blessed him. God said to him, 'Your name is Jacob; no longer shall you be called Jacob, but Israel shall be your name.' So he was called Israel. God said to him, 'I am El Shadday. Be fruitful and multiply; a nation and a community of nations shall come from you, and kings shall spring from you. The land that I gave to Abraham and Isaac, I will give to you, and I will give the land to your offspring after you.' Then God went up from him at the place where he had spoken with him. Jacob set up a pillar in the place where he had spoken with him, a pillar of stone; and he poured out a drink-offering on it and poured oil on it. So Jacob called the place where God had spoken with him Beth-El" (Genesis 35:9-15, P writer).

"What is YHWH your God asking from you except to fear YHWH, your God, to go in all His ways, and to love Him and to serve YHWH, your God with all your heart and all your soul, to observe YHWH's commandments and His laws" (Deuteronomy 10:12-14, Dtr1).

"These people draw near with their mouths and honor me with their lips, while their hearts are far from me, and their worship of me is a human commandment learned by rote" (Isaiah 29:13).

"Happy are those who consider the poor; the LORD delivers them in the day of trouble. The LORD protects them and keeps them alive; they are called happy in the land. You do not give them up to the will of their enemies. The Lord sustains them on their sickbed; in their illness, you heal all their infirmities." (Psalm 41:1-3)

"Fools say in their hearts, 'There is no God.' They are corrupt, they commit abominable acts; there is no one who does good. God looks down from heaven on humankind to see if there are any who are wise, who seek after God. They have all fallen away, they are all perverse; there is no one who does good, no, not one. Have they no knowledge, those evildoers, who eat up my people as they eat bread, and do not call upon God?" (Psalm 53:1-4).

"Praise the LORD! Praise God in his sanctuary; praise him in his mighty firmament! Praise him for his mighty deeds; praise him according to his surpassing greatness! Praise him with trumpet sound; praise him with lute and harp! Praise him with tambourine and dance; praise him with strings and pipe! Praise him with clanging cymbals; praise him with loud clashing cymbals! Let everything that breathes praise the LORD! Praise the LORD!" (Psalm 150:1-6).

A God Who Rewards Faithfulness. Even if others around you are laughing at you, you should be faithful to the One God, and you will be rewarded with prosperity. "Happy are those who do not follow the advice of the wicked, or take the path that sinners tread, or sit in the seat of scoffers; but their delight is in the law of the LORD, and on his law, they meditate day and night. They are like trees planted by streams of water, which yield their fruit in its season, and their leaves do not wither. In all that they do, they prosper" (Psalm 1:1-3).

A God Who Expects Self-Sacrifice. There are 249 verses in the Hebrew Bible where God demands sacrifice or where there was an expectation that God required it. In the BLUE vMeme, the sacrifice is no longer about animals. It is the act of self-discipline, required for the good of the whole community. "If a man is righteous and does what is lawful and right—if he does not eat upon the mountains or lift up his eyes to the idols of the house of Israel, does not defile his neighbor's wife or approach a woman during her menstrual period, does not oppress anyone, but restores to the debtor his pledge, commits no robbery, gives his bread to the hungry and covers the naked with a garment, does not take advance or accrued interest, withholds his hand from iniquity, executes true justice between contending parties, follows my statutes, and is careful to observe my ordinances, acting faithfully—such a one is righteous; he shall surely live, says YHWH" (Ezekiel 18:5-9). This emphasis on self-sacrifice, with a promised future reward, is a characteristic of an authoritarian worldview.

A God Who is the ultimate authority. What God says is the final word. He dictates his commands to the people. He commands respect. With this belief, the writers used simple phrases to remind the people of God's authority in their lives and to reinforce their words. In the book of Leviticus, many chapters begin with "And the LORD spoke to Moses, saying..." Sometimes the writer put this line in the middle of the paragraph. For example, concerning what animals can be eaten: "... You shall not defile yourselves with them, and so become unclean. For I am the LORD your God; sanctify yourselves therefore, and be holy, for I am holy." (Leviticus 11: 43b-44a P writer) The prophets would do the same, "The word that came to

Jeremiah from the Lord," (Jeremiah 7:1) and "Thus says the Lord:" (Isaiah 56:1) Such authoritarian phrases catch the attention and imbue the words with expectations of obedience.

A God Who Loves Justice: There is a divine paradox between justice and mercy. In RED, the people begged and sacrificed for mercy. In BLUE, they begin to understand that God acts with justice and expects humankind to love justice as well. This is a strong characteristic of the BLUE vMeme, as well as of the Axial Age. In the following verse, the writer is aware that the burnt offerings that were acceptable in the past are now meaningless. Sacrifice is now about personal devotion. One's consciousness must be contrite and humble.

"'With what shall I come before the Lord, and bow myself before God on high? Shall I come before him with burnt offerings, with calves a year old? Will the Lord be pleased with thousands of rams, with tens of thousands of rivers of oil? Shall I give my firstborn for my transgression, the fruit of my body for the sin of my soul?' He has told you, O mortal, what is good; and what does YHWH require of you but to do justice, and to love kindness, and to walk humbly with your God?" (Micah 6:6–8).

"YHWH, your God: He is the God of gods and the LORD of lords, the great YHWH, the mighty and the awesome God, who won't be partial and won't take a bribe, doing judgment for an orphan and a widow and loving an alien, to give him bread and a garment" (Deuteronomy 10:17. Dtr[1]).

"Now, let the fear of the LORD be upon you; take care what you do, for there is no perversion of justice with the LORD our God, or partiality, or taking of bribes" (2 Chronicles 19:7).

"He loves righteousness and justice; the earth is full of the steadfast love of the LORD" (Psalm 33:5).

"Seek good and not evil, that you may live; and so, the LORD, the God of hosts, will be with you, just as you have said. Hate evil and love good and establish justice in the gate; it may be that the LORD, the God of hosts, will be gracious to the remnant of Joseph. Therefore, thus says the LORD, the God of hosts, ... I hate, I despise your festivals, and I take no delight in your solemn assemblies. Even though you offer me your burnt offerings and grain offerings, I will not accept them; and the offerings of well-being of your fatted animals I will not look upon. Take away from me the noise of your songs; I will not listen to the melody of your harps. But let justice roll down like waters, and righteousness like an ever-flowing stream" (Amos 5:14-16a, 21--24).

"Learn to do good, devote yourselves to justice; aid the wronged, uphold the rights of the orphan; defend the cause of the widow continue to nourish humanity's pursuit of social justice" (Isaiah 1:17).

Other examples of a God who requires self-sacrifice can be found in the following passages: Psalm 37:28; Psalm 89:14; Psalm 119:149; Jeremiah 22:3-4; Zechariah 7:9-10; Amos 2:6-7.

A God Who Provides Law. The BLUE Absolutist worldview perceives that the laws that have been established for the governance of the people have come from the Lord. "See, just as the Lord my God has charged me, I now teach you statutes and ordinances for you to observe in the land that you are about to enter and occupy. You must observe them diligently, for this will show your wisdom and discernment to the peoples, who, when they hear all these statutes, will say, 'Surely this great nation is a wise and discerning people!' For what other great nation has a god so near to it as the Lord our God is whenever we call to him? And what other great nation has statutes and ordinances as just as this entire law that I am setting before you today?" (Deuteronomy 4: 5-8, Dtr1).

An Anthropomorphic God Who Makes Covenants with people. Covenants were formal, binding agreements that defined relationships and responsibilities between two or more parties. They required sacrifice and unquestioning obedience. For the first time in human awareness God is perceived to be loving, but as illustrated by the covenants with his chosen people it is conditional love.

God's contribution to the covenant starts with his requirement to be blameless. "When Abram was ninety-nine years old, the Lord appeared to Abram, and said to him, 'I am God Almighty. Walk before me and be blameless. And I will make my covenant between me and you and will make you exceedingly numerous. . ... This is my covenant with you: You shall be the ancestor of a multitude of nations. No longer shall your name be Abram, but your name shall be Abraham; for I have made you the ancestor of a multitude of nations. I will make you exceedingly fruitful, and I will make nations of you, and kings shall come from you. I will establish my covenant between me and you, and your offspring after you throughout their generations, for an everlasting covenant, to be God to you and to your offspring after you. And I will give to you, and to your offspring after you, the land where you are now an alien, all the land of Canaan, for a perpetual holding; and I will be their God'" (Genesis 17:1-8, P writer).

Abraham's contribution to the covenant. "God said to Abraham, 'As for you, you shall keep my covenant. . ... Every male among you shall be circumcised. . ... and it shall be a sign of the covenant between me and you. . ... So shall my covenant be in your flesh an everlasting covenant. Any uncircumcised male who is not circumcised in the flesh of his foreskin shall be cut off from his people; he has broken my covenant'" (Genesis 17:9-14, P writer).

Then God appeared to Abraham's grandson Jacob: "God appeared to Jacob, and he blessed him. God said to him, 'Your name is Jacob; no longer shall you be called Jacob, but Israel shall be your name.' So he was called Israel. God said to him, 'I am El Shadday. Be fruitful and multiply; a nation and a community of nations shall come from you, and kings shall spring from you. The land that I gave to Abraham and Isaac, I will give to you, and I will give the land to your offspring after you.' Then God went up from him at the place where he had spoken with him. Jacob set up a pillar in the place where he had spoken with him, a pillar of stone; and he poured out a drink-offering on it and poured oil on it. So Jacob called the place where God had spoken with him Beth-El" (Genesis 35:9-15, P writer).

A God Who Offers Conditional Love, and Conditional Blessings and Curses. The BLUE consciousness perceives a God who protects and provides for his people, but only if they are faithful. "The Lord will open for you his rich storehouse, ... and to bless all your undertakings. . .. if you obey the commandments of the Lord your God. But if you will not obey the Lord your God by diligently observing all his commandments and decrees . . . then all these curses shall come upon you and overtake you." (Deuteronomy 28:12-15, Dtr1).

"Cursed shall you be in the city and cursed shall you be in the field. . ..The Lord will send upon you disaster, panic, and frustration in everything you attempt to do, until you are destroyed and perish quickly, on account of the evil of your deeds, because you have forsaken me" (Deuteronomy 28:16, 20, Dtr1).

"If you return, O Israel, says YHWH, if you return to me, if you remove your abominations from my presence, and do not waver, and if you swear, 'As YHWH lives!' in truth, in justice, and in uprightness, then nations shall be blessed by him, and by him they shall boast" (Jeremiah 4:2, Dtr2).

"For if you truly amend your ways and your doings, if you truly act justly one with another, if you do not oppress the alien, the orphan, and the widow, or shed innocent blood in this place, and if you do not go after other gods to your own hurt, then I will dwell with you in this place, in the land that I gave of old to your ancestors forever and ever" (Jeremiah 7:5-7).

If you turn from God, He will turn away from you. If you return, God will be there. "Ever since the days of your ancestors you have turned aside from my statutes and have not kept them. Return to me, and I will return to you, says the LORD of hosts." (Malachi 3: 7)

A God Who is Loving but Vengeful. The J and E writers knew a god of vengeance, not one of love. The idea of a loving God emerged with the BLUE consciousness, but it combined with the RED vengeful God. In the BLUE worldview, one perceives the love of God as conditional. (loving and vengeful)

"For I, YHWH your God am a jealous God, punishing children

for the iniquity of parents, to the third and the fourth generation of those who reject me, but showing steadfast love to the thousandth generation of those who love me and keep my commandments" (Exodus 20:5-6, P writer).

"Vengeance is mine, and recompense" (Deuteronomy 32:35, D writer).

"If you continue hostile to me, and will not obey me, I will continue to plague you sevenfold for your sins. I will let loose wild animals against you, and they shall bereave you of your children and destroy your livestock; they shall make you few, and your roads shall be deserted" (Leviticus 26:21-22, P writer).

"Hear this, I pray you, you heads of the house of Jacob, and rulers of the house of Israel, that abhor justice, and pervert all equity. . . Assuredly, because of you, Zion shall be plowed as a field, and Jerusalem shall become heaps of ruins" (Micah 3:9-12).

A God Who Answers Prayer. God will answer prayers, but only the prayers of the righteous.

"When the righteous cry for help, the Lord hears and rescues them from all their troubles.: (Psalm 34:17)

"And the children of Israel groaned from the work, and they cried out, and their wail went up to God from the work. And God heard their moaning, and God remembered His covenant with Abraham, with Isaac, and with Jacob. And God saw the children of Israel. And God knew!" (Exodus 2:23b-25, P writer).

"For surely, I know the plans I have for you, says the Lord, plans for your welfare and not for harm, to give you a future with hope. . ... When you search for me, you will find me, if you seek me with all your heart" (Jeremiah 29:10).

"Call on me in the day of trouble; I will deliver you, and you shall glorify me" (Psalm 50:15).

A God Who Gives Comfort. The prophets arose each time the kingdoms experienced difficulties. They took on the job of warning the people, including the kings and priests, to return to the one true

God. The prophets generally criticized the people and condemned them to God's judgment in the form of droughts, floods, and invasions. But they also spoke hopeful words of a future of peace and prosperity.

As the BLUE consciousness matures, the (RED) perception of a petty, impetuous god fades, and God is perceived to be protective and supportive, a source of hope. We can see this more mature perception of God in the book of Isaiah. Isaiah calls the people to repent but he offers comfort and inspiration as well. God understands the people's grief over the destruction of their temple and the exile. His messengers bring comfort and hope.

"Comfort, O comfort my people, says your God. Speak tenderly to Jerusalem, and cry to her that she has served her term, that her penalty is paid, that she has received from the LORD's hand double for all her sins. . .. Have you not known? Have you not heard? YHWH is the everlasting God, the Creator of the ends of the earth. He does not faint or grow weary; his understanding is unsearchable. He gives power to the faint and strengthens the powerless. Even youths will faint and be weary, and the young will fall exhausted; but those who wait for the LORD shall renew their strength, they shall mount up with wings like eagles, they shall run and not be weary, they shall walk and not faint" (portions of Isaiah 40, Second Isaiah).

"You who live in the shelter of the Most High, who abide in the shadow of the Almighty, will say to the LORD, 'My refuge and my fortress; my God, in whom I trust.' For he will deliver you from the snare of the fowler and from the deadly pestilence; he will cover you with his pinions, and under his wings you will find refuge; his faithfulness is a shield and buckler. . .. For he will command his angels concerning you to guard you in all your ways. On their hands they will bear you up so that you will not dash your foot against a stone" (Psalm 91).

"They shall all sit under their own vines and under their own fig trees, and no one shall make them afraid . . . We will walk in the name of YHWH forever and ever" (Micah 4).

A God Who Favors his Own People. The Hebrew people knew that they were chosen and favored by their God. This is an essential concept in their perspective on the world.

"The Lord has chosen you out of all the peoples to be his people, his treasured possession" (Deuteronomy 7).

"Here, YHWH, your God, has the skies – and the skies of the skies! – the earth and everything that's in it. Only, YHWH was attracted to your fathers, to love them, and He chose their seed after them: you, out of all the people, as it is this day" (Deuteronomy 10:14).

"You shall be holy to me; for I am holy. I have separated you from the other peoples to be mine" (Leviticus 20).

"For the vineyard of YHWH is the house of Israel, and the people of Judah are his pleasant planting" (Isaiah 5:7)

A God Who is Patriarchal, masculine, and dominates by might. Earlier worldviews imagined a feminine figure in the pantheon of the gods, but in BLUE monotheism, the identity of the divine becomes masculine only.

"Has any people ever heard the voice of a god speaking out of a fire, as you have heard, and lived? Or has any god ever attempted to go and take a nation for himself from the midst of another nation, by trials, by signs and wonders, by war, by a mighty hand and an outstretched arm, and by terrifying displays of power, as the Lord your God did for you in Egypt before your very eyes?" (Deuteronomy 4:33-34. Dtr[1]).

"In the year that King Uzziah died, I saw the Lord sitting on a throne, high and lofty; and the hem of his robe filled the temple. Seraphs were in attendance above him; each had six wings: with two they covered their faces, and with two they covered their feet, and with two they flew. And one called to another and said: 'Holy, holy, holy is the Lord of hosts; the whole earth is full of his glory'" (Isaiah 6:1-3).

"To whom then will you compare me, or who is my equal? says the Holy One. Lift up your eyes on high and see: Who created these?

He who brings out their host and numbers them, calling them all by name; because he is great in strength, mighty in power" (Isaiah 40: 25-26).

"For lo, the one who forms the mountains creates the wind, reveals his thoughts to mortals, makes the morning darkness, and treads on the heights of the earth—YHWH, the God of hosts, is his name!" (Amos 4:13).

A God Who is Absolute, Unchanging, Timeless: In this worldview, God is timeless, consistent, and unchanging. He will make the same judgments now as in the past because God's law doesn't change.

"Before the mountains were brought forth, or ever you had formed the earth and the world, from everlasting to everlasting you are God" (Psalm 90:2).

"For I the Lord do not change" (Malachi 3:6).

Revisiting Three Prevalent Biblical Discrepancies

In this section, we will revisit the three discrepancies posited in Chapter 2, and comment on the worldview of the writers. This issue was also addressed in Chapter 5, where we considered the ancient purple/RED worldview.

The P Writer's Creation Myth

As mentioned, the Axial Age introduced significant development of culture, and written language matured significantly. This is obvious when we compare the two creation stories. In Genesis 1, the P writer's creation myth (circa late 8th century BCE) is far more organized and poetically eloquent than the J writer's creation story of Genesis 2. (circa 10th century BCE). Valuing order and discipline, with an emphasis on goodness and providence is highly indicative of the BLUE value system.

The P writer tells his story with deliberate order and poetic repetition. Through this style, he infers that the creator is transcendent and absolute. No longer is God impulsive and childlike. This all-powerful God merely says the word, and something comes into being. God is benevolent as indicated in his calling each day "good," and providing for the people. The writer declares that everything God has created is excellent.

The pre-modern worldviews (all stages before ORANGE) perceived a three-tiered universe: the flat plate of earth, the heaven or sky above, and the sea including the waters under the earth. This model was not a metaphor; to them, it was an unquestionable fact. Notice these three tiers in the creation story. The earth is a flat land mass either floating on the water (because water sometimes flows up from the ground) or is supported by pillars. The sea surrounds the land mass and was considered chaotic and dangerous. Below the earth was the home of the dead: a netherworld. The heavens consisted of two parts. The upper heavens were the domain of the deities. The lower heavens contained the stars, planets, sun, and moon. The sky was a solid dome that held back or allowed the rains to pass through.

The P Writer's Great Flood Myth

Genesis 6:9b-22, Genesis 7:8-9, 11, 13-16a, 21, 24, Genesis 8:1-2a, 3b-5, 7, 13a, 14-19, Genesis 9:1-17

When writing about the flood, the P writer maintains the pre-modern idea about the construct of the world. "And the fountains of the deep and the apertures of the skies were shut." (Genesis 8:2, P writer).

P begins his story by stating unequivocally that "Noah was a virtuous man." The P story does not mention anything negative about Noah, exhibiting BLUE's values of social appropriateness and guilt.

Like the J writer, P sees an anthropomorphic god. Although he emphasizes that the flood was a result of God's anger toward humanity, he also perceives a caring, protective God and uses the flood to explain why rainbows appear in the sky. "And God remembered Noah and all the wild animals and all the domestic animals that were with him in the ark, and God passed a wind over the earth, and the water decreased" (Genesis 8:1, P writer).

Typical of the BLUE value system, we find more intellectual sophistication and much attention to detail in P's flood story. The P writer provides YHWH's specific instructions regarding the materials and dimensions of the ark. In P's BLUE value system, animal sacrifice was no longer required, which is why the Priestly writer reports that YHWH required just one pair of each of the animals. P is aware of humankind's responsibility: YHWH told Noah to store food for the future.

Today's reader might wonder why the Redactor who wove together the stories of the Great Flood did not edit out the discrepancies between the J and the P documents. Modern (ORANGE) learners depend on differentiating fact from fiction. But this was not a concept before the Modern stage of consciousness. In other words, people did not care about mixing fact and fiction, as long as it delivered the message. We must not impose Modern values upon a stage of consciousness that did not have that awareness.

The P Writer's Ten Commandments.

The D writer's set of commandments was formed at the time of the exile, 586 BCE, centuries after Moses allegedly met YHWH on the mountain. The earlier commandments were tied to survival as tribal nomads, but the D writer's focus was on ethical and moral imperatives to maintain a civil society. Consistent with the shift into a more complex society, adherence to the latter set of commandments is tied to a less tangible reward than survival. God, the authoritarian who brought the Israelites out of bondage, commands respect and self-discipline. Immediately following the commandments, the writer reminds the reader about the covenant and God's transcendent power.

Both are typical characteristics of the authoritative BLUE vMeme. The writer concludes that Moses had the authority to convey God's requirements for the people (Deuteronomy 5:22-33).

Deuteronomy 5 (circa 600s BCE)

1. Have no other gods.
2. Make no idols.
3. Keep the sabbath holy.
4. No wrong use of God's name.
5. Honor father and mother.
6. You shall not murder.
7. You shall not commit adultery.
8. You shall not steal.
9. Bear no false witness.
10. Do not covet a neighbor's house or wife.

The traditional authoritarian BLUE worldview is present in every book of the Bible, including those that were discussed in our consideration of the PURPLE and RED worldview as well as some that are classified as Wisdom Writings.[54] BLUE is the predominant value system represented by the Hebrew religion; therefore, every book of Hebrew and Christian scripture represents a predominant worldview of the BLUE tradition.

The BLUE vMeme's Influence on Scripture and Religion

The BLUE authoritarian worldview established back in the days of Judah's King Josiah became the root value system of the Jewish and Christian understanding of God, sin, and redemption. The BLUE mythic worldview formed the idea of establishing "Sacred Scriptures," and the "Holy Bible." Years of BLUE church orthodoxy created a belief in the Bible's mystique. It accepts the words of the Bible with unquestioning obedience, calling it "holy." In the eyes of the religiously devout, any Bible ever published is revered as a sacred object. To doubt its message is a serious sin. So strong is the Bible's influence that people fear a terrible consequence (like being struck by lightning) if they dare question it, or if a person who holds a predominantly BLUE worldview drops their Bible on the floor, they might feel horrified! BLUE uses only the canonized scriptures to defend its beliefs, even if those beliefs defy science and logic. Typically, BLUE religious teachings are dictated by a lectionary that was determined by the authorities in the church. Sunday sermons are expected to be inspired by a Bible reference. Other ancient or contemporary sources are not acceptable sources of wisdom.

BLUE's religious mission to spread the good news of salvation to others is motivated by its belief that everyone must follow their exclusive path to God. This worldview also expects you to not apply reason or to ask questions. The answers are in the written "word of God," which is found exclusively in the canonical Scriptures.

For centuries, the BLUE Roman Catholic Church campaigned effectively to stop scholars from questioning the Bible, declaring heresy against anyone who questioned the scriptures. They deliberately withheld the actual teachings of the Bible from the parishioners. Contemporary BLUE American traditional Christianity continues a pre-modern religious defense of the mythic story. This worldview informs them that the Bible is the only inspired word of God, and they will defend this belief by using the Bible as proof. Most Christians remain unaware of the implications of what we have explained in this book. They are unaware that the gospel writers quoted Hebrew texts to create stories about Jesus.

From the beginning of the Jewish story of the 7th century BCE through to the Enlightenment of the late 17th century CE, the predominant worldview was the authoritarian BLUE. This worldview values precise rules, with obvious consequences if the rules are broken. BLUE religion threatens punishment from God if the rules are disobeyed. It enforces self-sacrifice and blind faith through fear. It sees humans as "broken," and depends on a savior or messiah for deliverance. BLUE is very well represented in the USA, but the last generation that was predominantly BLUE was the WWII or "Silent" Generation. If a person does not adhere to the rules of the BLUE faith and steps off the path they can be subject to discipline by the church elders or social pressures like shunning. Readers from all generations will have personal experiences with this BLUE way of keeping everyone in conformity. This is the way Judaism and Christianity were defined.

Don't Skip This Section! Interesting thoughts, anecdotes, and prompts for discussion.

(The numbers before each item are for reference only and do not indicate suggested order or importance.)

1. Read and Reflect: Choose one of the prophets that describe the Transition Period: the time of the Judges: Elijah in 1 Kings, 2 Kings; Elisha in 2 Kings; Nathan in 2 Samuel 7 and 12, 1 Kings 1; 1st Isaiah in Isaiah 1-39, Hosea, Micah, Nahum, Habakkuk, Zephaniah. Read enough of the scripture to get a good sense of the tone, style, message, etc. What behaviors, comments, and attitudes reveal the RED consciousness? What do the prophets say that suggests a call to BLUE consciousness? Consider the prophets' call for social reform (from RED to BLUE). How does this message compare with the shift from ORANGE to GREEN we're experiencing in the twenty-first century CE? (If you are studying with a group, choose different prophets and report back in the next session).

2. Read and Reflect: Choose one of the prophets from the exile or post-exilic period: Obadiah, Second Isaiah. Jeremiah, Third Isaiah, Joel, Haggai, Zechariah, Malachi. Read enough of the scripture to get a good sense of the tone, style, message, etc. What specific behaviors is the prophet pinpointing? What new behaviors are suggested? What does

he say that indicates a call for RED to shift into the BLUE worldview? This transition is a major shift in consciousness that took centuries to manifest. Reflect on how shift causes chaos before resolution. Apply your ideas to the societal chaos occurring in the twenty-first century. Share your observations and insights.

3. Learn more: The kings of the divided kingdom are a topic of great research. Check out the *History in The Bible* website by Gary Stevens for charts and podcasts. www.historyinthebible. com Timeline of the Two Kingdoms, Chart of the Kings

4. Consider perspective: You may have noticed that the exile lasted "only" about 80 years. Of course, it's all about perspective. As we look back at this ancient history, we consider these periods to be relatively short. The monarchy, the long-awaited "Kingdom of God in the Promised Land," lasted only one hundred years. After the kingdom split, Israel lasted only two hundred years. And the exile was not the final event and didn't last forever, although the people must have felt that way at the time. Also, consider thesis, antithesis, and synthesis: The Judeans had enjoyed many generations developing a proud religious and ethnic identity (thesis). Then life conditions changed, and the thesis was met with an antithesis—the exile to Babylon. "How can we sing the Lord's song in a foreign land?" (Psalm 137) The exile was a complete loss or death of the old paradigm (antithesis), and it spanned about two generations, long enough to experience the chaos or void required to re-frame the dilemma. Long enough to bring up a new generation of leaders who could envision how to lead with greater understanding and wisdom. In the process of shifting from one paradigm to another, the "wilderness experience" of crisis and chaos is a necessary passage, a "crucifixion," that allows us to release unhealthy shadows from our collective consciousness. Through that experience, we make way for synthesis, a "resurrection"

into the new paradigm of a greater good. Karen Armstrong wrote, "Even the Jews, who had suffered so horribly from the imperial adventures in the Middle East, had been propelled into their Axial Age by the terrifying freedom that had followed the destruction of their homeland and the trauma of deportation that severed their link with the past and forced them to start again."[55]

5. Apply this lesson to the situation in the United States in 2021. Will a "wilderness experience" like this one be the catalyst for us to birth a greater reality? The United States constitution is 225 years old. Written in the eighteenth century, portions of it do not anticipate the paradigm of the twenty-first century (i.e., Supreme Court justices appointed for life. In 1782, when the constitution was created, life expectancy was 39.5 years.) Reform likely won't happen without a significant catalyst, a "crucifixion experience" that shakes things up. Two generations suffered exile in the sixth century BCE. Will the present transformation take two generations? Spiral Dynamics says most likely not. We are much more flexible and knowledgeable than the people of that time. Our creativity is keen, and our attitudes are global. Our synthesis (our collective shift into the next vMeme) will come swiftly.

6. Apply: In this chapter, we read, "The theme from the Torah continues into the Prophets: life is a cycle of covenant, infidelity, defeat (punishment) and repentance and forgiveness/redemption." Apply this idea to your personal, spiritual, and emotional evolution. This is also comparable to the idea of thesis, antithesis, and synthesis. When we're ready to shift into a more expansive worldview, we often experience unhealthy manifestations of our current level of consciousness. Behaviors and attitudes of the past now seem to be ineffective and frustrating. We can feel that we are in a "wilderness experience" of misery, discontent, and imbalance. When we can break through the discontent or

push through that disorienting chaos into a more expansive worldview, it's like a rebirth; we feel the peace of resolution. It feels like redemption. This happens in both the individual and collective consciousness. Consider how an event in your life illustrates this cycle.

Chapter 7

An Intelligent God: The Wisdom Writings

"To get wisdom is to love oneself; to keep understanding is to prosper." Proverbs 19:8

In contrast to the books that we have already visited, which focus on cultural history, prophecies and law, the Wisdom literature is the voice of everyday existence: how we live, learn, love, and cope in the day-to-day struggles and joys of life. Wisdom literature gives clues into the consciousness of humanity, portraying philosophy, curiosity, and reason expressed mostly during the Second Temple Period. The Prophetic period had ended. The Second Temple period writings consist of love poems, songs, satire, short stories, metaphors, parables, morality myths, apocalyptic literature, and existential discourse.

Historical Context

The Second Temple Period covers the time following the Babylonian exile when they rebuilt the Temple (thus the name), through 70 CE when Romans destroyed the Second Temple. Like the prior periods, the Second Temple Period represents another six hundred years of cultural, systemic, intellectual, and spiritual evolution. During this set of six hundred years, the Jewish identity evolved into a nation with its footing on the international stage.

The Babylonian Period (586-516 BCE)

Babylonian forces overtook Assyrian land, including Judah. With the temple and the entire holy city destroyed, and the leaders and elite class exiled to Babylon, the remaining people were left to scratch out a living in the countryside. Meanwhile, the elites found themselves immersed in a foreign culture: "By the rivers of Babylon, there we sat down and there we wept when we remembered Zion. On the willows there we hung up our harps. For there, our captors asked us for songs, and our tormentors asked for mirth, saying, 'Sing us one of the songs of Zion!' How could we sing the LORD's song in a foreign land?" (Psalm 137:1-4).

The destruction of their homeland was a major life event that paved the way for a theological and societal shift. The Second Temple Period introduced cultural influences from three major powers: the Persian Empire, the Greek Empire (Hellenistic period), and the Roman Empire. (The books of Jeremiah and Lamentations were written during the Exile.)

The Persian Period (516-332 BCE)

Persian King Cyrus conquered the Babylonian empire in 538 BCE and decreed that the Jews must return to their homeland. A priest scribe and a building foreman named Ezra and Nehemiah rallied the Jewish elites to leave a relatively good life in Babylon and rebuild the temple, repair the walls of Jerusalem, and form a new theistic government that defined a distinctly Jewish identity. The governance they established was a unique theocracy combining and centralizing the seat of religion and justice. And, while captive in Babylon, they learned Zoroastrian ideas, which influenced Second Temple Judaism and eventually made a strong impact on Christian thinking. (2nd Isaiah wrote during this period, and laws against intermarriage were established in the new Jerusalem.)

The Hellenistic Period (332–63 BCE)

Following the conquests of Alexander the Great, Hellenistic culture influenced Jewish thought. Classical Greek philosophers explored rationalistic concepts concerning absolute and changing reality, four basic elements of the universe, and the phenomenon of paradoxes. These concepts infiltrated Jewish (and later, Christian) theology. Modern Hellenism had introduced liberal and cosmopolitan policies which conservatives feared threatened their religious identity. Dozens of Hebrew sects such as the Pharisees, Sadducees, Essenes, and Zealots formed during the Persian and Hellenistic periods, influenced by Zoroastrianism (aka Mazdeism) and Greek culture. Simultaneously, Socrates expressed his ideas of moral philosophy. The Hebrew Scriptures were translated into Koine Greek, which was adopted by Greek-speaking Jews.[56] As a result, during this period, the Jewish community developed diverse sectarian facets, and cohesion of the Jewish community was seriously lacking.

As the Hellenistic presence in the Levant waned and Roman influence gathered strength, one Jewish sect rose in revolt. The full story of this Maccabean Revolt is recorded in First and Second Maccabees (non-canonical books [57]). The Maccabees established an independent kingdom from about 110 to 63 BCE. They were a pious group (RED/BLUE) that rose to resist the influence of Hellenism (BLUE/ORANGE).

For fifty years they managed to reestablish the authority of the Jewish religion. They succeeded in some battles to expand the territory of Judah, but they were summarily stopped by the power of Rome. (The books of Proverbs, Ecclesiastes, Job, Song of Songs, and some of the Psalms were written during this period.

The Roman Period (63 BCE– 324 CE)

After years of Jewish defiance against foreign-imposed laws, taxation, standards, and practices, Rome exerted its dominance and quashed the Jewish insurrection, destroying the temple for a second time and ending the Second Temple Period in 70 CE. A major point of tension between Rome and the Jews (and the Jewish population in the Jesus movement) was polytheism vs. monotheism. While Jews thought it heresy to revere any god but YHWH, the Romans considered it blasphemy not to revere all the gods, and treasonous not to bow to Caesar, son of the gods. Both positions come from a BLUE value system. (The books of Esther, Daniel, and the books of the Maccabees and Sirach were written during the Roman period.)

The Bible books considered in this chapter are Job, Proverbs, Ecclesiastes, Song of Songs, Esther, Ruth, Daniel, and Jonah.

Wisdom Writings That Display the BLUE Authoritarian Worldview

The Psalms, considered part of the Wisdom Writings, are a collection of poems, songs, and reflections from King David to the late Second Temple Period, and they contain varying perceptions of God and humankind. As mentioned in Chapter 5, King David's psalms convey his RED worldview. He prayed to his warrior God for protection and deliverance when he was hiding from Saul. (Psalm 57 and 59; Psalm 110: 5-6) The Psalms also portray characteristics of the BLUE vMeme: congregational songs of praise and celebration, and poems of faith and comfort, mostly out of the BLUE worldview, where we perceive a righteous fair god who rewards the faithful, and we hear a call to a cooperative society. "How very good and pleasant it is when kindred live together in unity!" (Psalm 133:1)

"Hear O my people, and I will speak O Israel, I will testify against you. I am God, your God. ... Those who bring thanksgiving as their sacrifice honor me; to those who go the right way, I will show the salvation of God. (Psalms 50:7, 22-23)

The book of Proverbs contains many references to values of authoritarian BLUE: "Those who spare the rod hate their children, but those who love them are diligent to discipline them" (Proverbs 13:24). Proverbs 25-29 are called "the proverbs of Solomon that the Officials of King Hezekiah of Judah copied." (Proverbs 25:1) In other words, these proverbs originated during the P writer's era. They represent BLUE values. They contain bits of common sense that would represent the "Right Living" value of BLUE. "What your eye have seen do not hastily bring into court; for what will you do in the end when your neighbor puts you to shame? Argue your case with your neighbor directly and do not disclose another's secret..." (Proverbs 25:8-9)

"Those who forsake the law praise the wicked, but those who keep the law struggle against them. The evil do not understand justice, but those who seek the Lord understand it completely." (Proverbs 28:4-5)

"The LORD possessed me in the beginning of his way, before his works of old" (Proverbs 8:22).

"Wisdom will come into your heart, and knowledge will be pleasant to your soul; It will save you from the way of evil, from those who speak perversely" (Proverbs 2:10-12).

"The path of the righteous is like the light of dawn, which shines brighter and brighter until full day. The way of the wicked is like deep darkness; they do not know what they stumble over" (Proverbs 4:18).

The wisdom books of Job (pronounced "Jobe") and Daniel include some Zoroastrian ideas that did not appear in Hebrew writings before the exile. Zoroastrianism has a vivid sense of dualism: Like the Hebrew YHWH, Ahura Mazda is a supreme God of order, wisdom, and justice. Zoroastrianism teaches that there is also Ahriman, an equal, hostile spirit, an absolute from the beginning of time, who must be destroyed. The faithful must pray to liberate the world from this hostile spirit. Eventually, a final apocalyptic judgment battle will result in ultimate cosmic peace. While the people were in exile in Babylon, these concepts influenced Jewish thought, introducing the ideas of Satan, hell, and apocalyptic times into their literature.

The book of Daniel (written in the second century BCE) is often classified as a book of a prophet, but scholars have found it to be full of invented events. It is literary fiction written with the magic of PURPLE and the devotion of BLUE with a RED apocalyptic message. The messages were highly influenced by Zoroastrianism. The first half of the book presents Daniel as a faithful follower of YHWH, who while in exile in Babylon during the 6th century, was unwilling to eat defiled food, and willing to suffer the consequences. Daniel is twice protected from death by fire and lions through the presence of YHWH's angels. He interprets dreams and mysterious writings on the wall that predict Nebuchadnezzar's fate. (Not exactly a prediction, since the story is set four hundred years before it was written.) The second half of the book of Daniel is apocalyptic (referring to end times), using mystical signs. Apocalyptic visions proclaim that God will reveal secret knowledge to certain people who are pious and have visionary powers. They are written in anticipation of the end of the world and that God will initiate a new beginning - the "Kingdom of God." The book of Job was written just before the Maccabean revolt (167-141 BCE), which is the only time Israel was a sovereign nation during the Second Temple Period.

Seeds of Consciousness:

As mentioned in earlier chapters, within every stage of the collective consciousness, unique voices express ideas that are way ahead of their time. For example, the Wisdom Writings were written during the Second Temple Period when Hellenism, Greek's Golden Age of philosophy and mathematics, was spreading east from Greece. This is a short-lived burst of awakening into the new world of reasoning and independent thinking of the ORANGE vMeme which won't become prevalent until The Enlightenment two thousand years later. Hellenism's seeds of consciousness naturally impressed upon the worldview of writers in the Middle East. These writings, which express humanistic, existential, reflective, and knowledge-oriented thinking, provide glimpses of the modern ORANGE consciousness. These early seeds of the ORANGE worldview would need centuries to develop, take root, and finally become a dominant value system. (Read more about the ORANGE vMeme in the Appendix)

Wisdom Writings Displaying ORANGE Modern Worldview

Due to the use of Persian terms and the development of Zoroastrian concepts, many scholars place the book of Job in the late 5th century or the 4th century BCE. Job is a complex morality story and fascinating philosophical fiction, written when the Greek philosophers were playing around with the ideas of Absolute and changing reality, and the phenomenon of paradoxes such as the kosmos, an ordered arrangement that cannot be understood via rational inquiry.[58] The Job story tells of a deal made between God and Satan "the Accuser" to see if Job will be faithful to God even if all his wealth and health were to be taken from him. This interaction emphasizes the BLUE Authoritarian value of devotion and the belief that God puts us to the test to see if we will be faithful. Some of Job's lines, however, express some pretty skeptical thoughts, inserting a bit of Greek rationalism and existentialism.

"Then the Lord answered Job out of the whirlwind: 'Who is this that darkens counsel by words without knowledge? Gird up your loins like a man, I will question you, and you shall declare to me. Where were you when I laid the foundation of the earth? Who determined its measurements—surely you know! Or who stretched the line upon it? On what were its bases sunk, or who laid its cornerstone when the morning stars sang together, and all the heavenly beings shouted for joy?'" (Job 38:1-7)

Proverbs, Ecclesiastes, and the Song of Songs were traditionally attributed to King Solomon, David's son because he was known for his wisdom. (The story in 1 Kings 3 reporting how Solomon acquired wisdom was created centuries after Solomon's reign. It is the first story about Solomon after the end of the J writer's novella.) These books contain wise ideas, far more complex and rational than the predominant consciousness of the time. In these passages, we can detect the dawning of ORANGE values.

The book of Ecclesiastes was written during the fourth through third centuries BCE. Ecclesiastes' literary form is a fictional autobiography: someone from the elite class relating his experiences and drawing lessons from them. In Ecclesiastes the author calls himself Qoheleth, meaning assembler, but this name is often translated as "preacher" or "teacher." He ponders the usefulness of living if we don't have enjoyment in doing so, indicating seeds of the ORANGE vMeme. But some of this writer's ideas speak of 2nd Tier awareness: the enjoyment of "being."

Plato's ideas regarding the nature of reality influenced these writings. Plato taught that everything we see in this realm is relative or not permanent. "Vanity of vanities! All is vanity. What do people gain from all the toil at which they toil under the sun?" (Ecclesiastes 1:2-3). Contextually, the word "vanity" (*hevel*) means "vapor" or "breath." In other words, the actions of man are temporal, not "real." Wisdom comes out of knowing that everything will eventually fade away. (This verse is a seed of 2nd Tier consciousness. It understands that the "having and doing" of the 1st Tier is meaningless.)

"There is an evil that I have seen under the sun, and it lies heavy upon humankind: those to whom God gives wealth, possessions, and honor so that they lack nothing of all that they desire, yet . . . does not . . . enjoy these things, but a stranger enjoys them. This is vanity; it is a grievous ill. A man may beget a hundred children and live many years, but however many are the days of his years if he does not enjoy life's good things . . . I say that a stillborn child is better off than he, for it comes into vanity and goes into darkness, . . . yet it finds rest rather than he. Even though he should live a thousand years twice over, yet enjoy no good—do not all go to one place?" (Ecclesiastes 6:1-6).

"For everything there is a season, and a time for every matter under heaven: a time to be born, and a time to die; a time to plant, and a time to pluck up what is planted; . . . What gain have the workers from their toil?. . I know that there is nothing better for them than to be happy and enjoy themselves as long as they live; moreover, it is God's gift that all should eat and drink and take pleasure in all their toil. I know that whatever God does endures forever; nothing can be added to it, nor anything taken from it" (Ecclesiastes 3:1-2, 9, 12-14).

The book of Proverbs is a collection written over hundreds of years. Wisdom is highly valued in many of the passages in Proverbs and Ecclesiastes. Central to the Greek ideas of the same period, Wisdom is personified as a divine feminine figure, Sophia. ("Philosophy" comes from the Greek words *philo* which means "to love" and *Sophia* which means "Wisdom"). Chapter after chapter describes and extolls the value of honoring Sophia, Wisdom.

"Happy are those who find wisdom, and those who get understanding, for her income is better than silver, and her revenue better than gold. She is more precious than jewels, and nothing you desire can compare with her. Long life is in her right hand; in her left hand are riches and honor. Her ways are ways of pleasantness, and all her paths are peace. She is a tree of life to those who lay hold of her; those who hold her fast are called happy" (Proverbs 3:13-18). Notice the value being placed on money, desire, and honor. These are ORANGE values, and they are less important than Wisdom.

The book of Proverbs contains thoughts that suggest the writer has awoken to a new worldview that seems to see a bigger picture than the norm: "Wisdom cries out in the street; .... at the entrance of the city gates, she speaks, 'How long, O simple ones, will you love being simple?'" (Proverbs 1:20-21).

The book of Esther is a short story set at the time it was written, during the reign of Persia's King Xerxes I, 486-465 BCE. The fictional story begins with Queen Vashti who has become an icon for feminist courage (ORANGE). Her actions are far removed from the value system of her husband and the Persian kingdom (RED/ BLUE). The replacement queen is a Hebrew orphan named Esther, who knew how to work within that structure to manipulate the king and save the Jews from the king's threat of ethnic cleansing. Esther and Mordecai display seeds of ORANGE through their creative, independent strategy that helps them win the game. This heroic tale is the reason for the celebratory Jewish festival of Purim.

Wisdom Writings that Display Seeds of the GREEN Post-Modern Worldview

The poetic pieces of the Wisdom Writings display seeds of consciousness of the GREEN vMeme. For example, they illustrate unprecedented moments of sensitivity and humanistic compassion. As mentioned in Chapter 4, Esau and Joseph display surprising acts of forgiveness that are way ahead of their time. (Genesis 33). (Acts of unconditional forgiveness are attempted in GREEN consciousness; they are foreign to the RED or BLUE concept of justice.)

Throughout human evolution, we have lovingly personified "Wisdom." Wisdom poses existential questions and invites practical perspectives on life. It suggests "two paths' That we can follow: one will lead to suffering and the other to well-being. Wisdom guides us on the path into oneness consciousness, and if true, it speaks to every level of consciousness in the Spiral. Each listener will take what wisdom they can hear from the passage.

Song of Songs (aka Song of Solomon) was traditionally dated from the tenth century because the first verse declares the book to be written by Solomon. "The Song of Songs, which is Solomon's." (Song of Songs 1:1) However, it contains vocabulary from the Persian, Greek, and Aramaic languages that are otherwise unknown in biblical Hebrew, indicating that it was written in the fourth or third centuries BCE. Song of Songs is a unique voice within the Hebrew Scriptures. Unlike the other books in the canon, it doesn't teach the law and covenant, it doesn't record history, and it doesn't appear to explain God's relationship to his people. It is unique from all the other books of the Bible: it celebrates a sensual love relationship and speaks of love with a tenderness that the earlier vMemes could not have expressed. We can see emergent ideas about women through the voices of two lovers. A woman speaks over half of the lines, and her voice is not filtered through a patriarchal narrator. These voices celebrate love and sexual desire, like the Greek's veneration of Eros. This interaction between a man and a woman is a sharp contrast to the way the earlier writers viewed women.

[The Man's Voice:] "I compare you, my love, to a mare among Pharaoh's chariots. Your cheeks are comely with ornaments, your neck with strings of jewels. We will make you ornaments of gold, studded with silver. . ... Ah, you are beautiful, my love; ah, you are beautiful; your eyes are doves. Ah, you are beautiful, my beloved, truly lovely" (Song of Songs 1:9-11, 16).

[The Woman's Voice:] "The voice of my beloved! Look, he comes, leaping upon the mountains, bounding over the hills. My beloved is like a gazelle or a young stag. . ... My beloved speaks and says to me: 'Arise, my love, my fair one, and come away; for now, the winter is past, the rain is over and gone. The flowers appear on the earth; the time of singing has come, and the voice of the turtle-dove is heard in our land" (Song of Songs 2: 8-12).

Reading Song of Songs as symbolic literature, we can apply the words to human relationships of all kinds. The book can also represent the mystical relationship between humankind and the divine. Jewish tradition considers it an allegory of the relationship between God and Israel. Some Christians interpret it as the relationship between Christ and his "bride," the church.

The book of Jonah is traditionally classified as one of the books of the prophets, but it more closely resembles one of the Wisdom Writings because it does not contain the message of a prophet; it is morality fiction with a prophet as the main character. The book is set in the eighth century BCE when Assyria dominated the region, but it was written four hundred years later. It tells the story of a prophet who was called to warn Assyria's capital city of Nineveh, to repent and turn to YHWH. It is sprinkled with relatable human behaviors, frank conversations with God, thrilling adventures on stormy seas, and scientifically impossible situations. As a great story often does, it ends with an unexpected leap of consciousness into the compassionate, inclusive GREEN worldview: God declares that he loves the people of Nineveh simply because they are his creation.

The book of Ruth is a short story about Naomi and her daughter-in-law Ruth, set in the tenth century BCE at the time of Samuel, the priest who anointed Saul, the first king of the monarchy. This is why the book is placed soon after the Torah (8th of 39 books of the Hebrew Bible). But this story was most likely created after the exile when intermarriage had become a point of contention. Many of the Jews who had remained in Judah during the exile had married non-Jews. Later, the returning exiled priests ruled against such marriages. With that political issue in mind, this story can be read as a political parable relating to the practicality of intermarriage. The thrust of the story hints at GREEN racial tolerance and inclusivity, a big leap from the tribal exclusivity of the times in which it is set.

We could read the Book of Ruth as an allegory, a hero's journey in the way of Jung, which features a woman as the hero! We can see that each element in the story represents the full spectrum of the 1st Tier. It is exciting to imagine that the creator of this story might have envisioned it from an exhilarating 2nd Tier integral state of consciousness.

Processing This Chapter

(The numbers do not indicate suggested order or importance.)

1. Read and Reflect: Choose to read one of these books: Proverbs, Job, Lamentations, Ecclesiastes, Esther, Ruth, or Jonah. You may skim some parts, but you'll want to read others more carefully. Look for any message that conveys seeds of consciousness beyond BLUE. It might be in one character, a quote, or the gist of the story. How is the tone different from the writings of the prophets? What do you see as the theme or main message? What Meme is represented? Explain. If you chose to study Ruth, see if you can decipher all 6 levels of the 1st Tier in the story, as mentioned above.

2. Consider and compare BLUE to ORANGE regarding Wisdom. If BLUE values Wisdom, it is about the wisdom of obedience. The way Wisdom is portrayed in Proverbs, is an independent thought process. Discuss why this is more of an ORANGE concept than a BLUE concept.

3. Learn more: Watch YouTube's *Crash Course in Jewish History— Session 8: The Second Temple Period*, August 2011 https://youtu.be/voi_etufV7Y

4. Learn more: Purim is likely the most fun festival of the Jewish calendar since Jews reenact the story with costumes. Watch YouTube's *What is Purim? An introduction to the Jewish holiday*, March 2017 https://youtu.be/6mmZDYogjCk

5. Apply: Consider how the Bible has influenced culture. Read Esther 1:22. The king sent a letter out to the entire kingdom declaring that "every man should be master in his own house." This phrase has been quoted throughout many generations, but few realize it is from the Bible. It can be used as a proof-text that God doesn't want women to be in charge, and that men have the right to teach their women what that means. Consider how this phrase played out in your family system. Apply what you know about Spiral Dynamics to gain insight into your social, emotional, and spiritual evolution. (You might start humming the song "Master of the House," from *Les Misérables* while thinking about this one.)

Chapter 8:

Integral Thinking About the Bible

As we read in Chapter One, H. Emilie Cady uses the phrase "the stupendous whole" to describe the essence of what is beyond the wall: Oneness; the Divine, The Whole of the Universe, "God." The wall and everything on this side of the wall comprises the relative world, and we think it's all that there is. Human beings have bought into an illusion that there is a big barrier between us and the Oneness; that we are separate from God and separate from others. When we can arrive at the Truth: that we are not separate and we are one unit, we are seeing "the stupendous whole."

About the person who said, 'I alone see the whole world,' Cady continues with her story, "He boldly proclaims, 'I have Truth; the others are in error, too orthodox,' and thus he calls the world's attention to the small size of the aperture through which he is looking at the stupendous whole. . .. Were it not at times so utterly ridiculous, it would always be pitiful to see the human mind of man trying to limit God to personal comprehension. Every time you try to limit God's manifestation of Himself in any person or through any person, in order to make that manifestation conform to what you see as Truth, you are only crying loudly: 'Ho! everyone, come and view my narrowness and my ignorance!'"

Cady understands how some people came to that outlook, but she bluntly calls it narrow-minded. "However much any one of us may know of God, there will always be unexplored fields in the realms of expression, and it is evidence of our narrow vision to say: 'This is all there is of God.' Beloved, as surely as you and I live, it is all one and the same Truth. There may be a distinction, but it is without difference."

Emilie Cady's story and her concluding words display an "integral" (Second Tier) point of view: Cady can see that everyone's worldview is legitimate, based on the size of their aperture. We begin with an exceedingly limited worldview and evolve our "picture" of God as we increase the aperture of our worldview. The integral view knows that one picture of God is not better than another. Some are more expansive than others, but they are all legitimate. Cady doesn't condemn the earlier ways to know God, not even the ancient PURPLE perception of God, which had been labeled "evil" and "savage" by generations of righteous religious people. She writes, "At the center, all is one and the same God. . ... He who worships the golden calf as his highest conception of God worships God. His mind has not yet expanded to a state where he can grasp any idea of God apart from a visible form, something that he can see with human eyes and handle with fleshly hands. But at heart he is seeking something higher than his present conscious self to be his deliverance out of evil."[59]

When a person can appreciate each of the previous worldviews without condemnation, that person is exhibiting Second Tier integral thinking.

Perception of God through the First Tier of the Spiral

Keeping this integral view in mind, we will revisit each level of the first 8 stages (the First Tier plus the first two levels of the Second Tier) to imagine how each worldview would answer this question: What is God and what am I in relation to God? We will consider how each vMeme might fill in these blanks: "God is _____, I am _____" and we will explain how people today apply these various worldviews to the Bible and their religious or spiritual thinking.

"God is ... I am ...." through the Spiral

The PURPLE vMeme has a magical perception of God. A person whose consciousness is centered in PURPLE might fill in the blanks listed above as: "God is <u>invisible spirits.</u> I am <u>in fear and awe of them.</u>" The PURPLE consciousness has a mystical outlook on life and is attuned to the natural nuances of the spirit world. The divine speaks through signs, angels, and visions.

We can integrate healthy PURPLE values into a contemporary experience of life through rituals or ceremonies that represent our awareness of the mystical Presence. Ritual ceremonies such as the Eucharist, baptism, christening, or ritual blessings and cleansings, sound healing, temporal rites, a passage into adulthood, and the White Stone and Burning Bowl ceremonies (favorites of the Unity movement) satisfy an innate desire to express mystical awareness in a visceral way that refreshes the spiritual seeker. Integration of PURPLE includes honoring and belonging to family or tribe, whatever form that takes in the 21st century.

Some people engage a PURPLE worldview when they treat scripture as a mysterious source of wisdom: they have a question, then they open the scripture to any passage and expect God will give them the answer through what they read. This worldview is also honored when someone uses crystals, Tarot cards, and other mystical devices in spiritual practices.

The RED vMeme

The RED vMeme has an egocentric, warrior perception of God. A person whose consciousness is centered in RED would fill in the blanks as follows: "God is <u>a warrior.</u> I am <u>his loyal soldier.</u>" Or "God is <u>a fickle manipulator.</u> I am <u>at the mercy of his whims.</u>" Consider King David's positive and negative characteristics. He was the hero of the RED consciousness in the Bible. Or think of Lt. Dan in the movie Forrest Gump, riding out the hurricane at the top of the sailboat's mast, daring God to come and take him. In RED consciousness, God is perceived as a strong warrior, determined to be the victor. God can crush his enemies and will protect his own. He confuses, frightens, and scatters the people when they attempt to gain too much power or control.

RED beliefs about God and the Bible are active in today's world. From football game prayers for victory to radical fundamentalist theology, the warrior God is called upon to support and justify their side. People who have a predominantly RED worldview perceive the Bible as the story of a divine heroic leader in a battle against evil. God will ensure the safety of his people through physical might and expects loyalty in return.

The BLUE vMeme

The BLUE vMeme has a monotheistic, authoritarian, mythical perception of God. In today's society, we see BLUE in the traditional, orthodox, or conservative religious view of God. A person whose consciousness is centered in BLUE would fill in the blanks as follows: "God is in charge and commands respect. I am (we are) His faithful servants." Or "God is the one who takes care of me if I'm obedient. I am His."

The BLUE cooperative consciousness values obedience to a Father-figure: a benevolent guardian God. In the BLUE perception of the divine, it is necessary to be humble and to live rightly. This God wants a relationship, not ritual appeasement, or radical crusades. We belong to God, and He takes care of us. In return, we are faithful to the teachings: submit our ego to God, accept his salvation, and we will find peace.

The ethnocentric BLUE Authoritarian worldview, being pre-rational, mythic, and patriarchal, established the concept of "Lord God" (like the lord of a manor or the master of the house) who has ultimate authority and whose word provides the only path of righteousness (right living). He is often personified as an authoritarian judge looking down upon you, or the Santa Claus God who gives you things when you ask, but only if you've been good.

The mythic worldview deems the written canonized Scriptures as the sole source of knowledge of God and exempts all other literature from the title of "inspired word of God." The following verse supports this viewpoint: "All scripture is given by inspiration of God, and is profitable for doctrine, for reproof, for correction, for instruction in righteousness" (2 Timothy 3:16 written in the 2nd century CE when the process of canonization was going on in the BLUE early Christian church.) The BLUE vMeme accepts this declaration as absolute truth.

The ORANGE vMeme

The ORANGE Modern vMeme has a perception of God that comes from a rational, scientific worldview. A person whose consciousness is centered in ORANGE would fill in the blanks as follows: "God is Principle and Law. I can harness It to create an enjoyable prosperous life."

For the first time in human conception, ORANGE dismisses the idea of a personified deity. "God" is energy, principle, and law. Modern spiritual seekers often substitute the name "God" with alternate words such as "First Cause," "Divine Mind," and "Source" to indicate that they are not referring to the mythic idea of the divine. The ORANGE God is the prime "unmoved mover" of everything in the universe, recognized in nature and reason. (This was a concept advanced by Aristotle as a primary cause.) This "First Cause" requires no dogma and has no interest in perpetuating religion. ORANGE rejects traditional religion as guilt-based, closed-minded, and needlessly rule-oriented. ORANGE theology is individualistic and humanistic, featuring the power of mind action and positive thinking, human potential, and prosperity teachings.

Modern consciousness was the catalyst for the protestant reformation. Martin Luther and John Calvin, while quite BLUE

Authoritarian in their theology, introduced ORANGE Modern thinking when they asserted that the people should be able to read in their spoken language and apply the Bible on their own.

ORANGE Bible readers and scholars reject the idea that the scriptures are directly inspired by God. They permit themselves to critique the Bible, find its origins, and dispel the myths of the traditional religion. Modern readers approach the Bible as literature that portrays past perspectives about God, therefore they have the freedom to paraphrase the Bible, choose the verses that appeal to them, and dispose of the rest or re-interpret the book with a metaphysical or maieutic approach. Some Modernists reject the value of scripture altogether and they don't expect the Sunday lesson to be based on a Bible quotation.

"New Thought," which arose in the USA in the 19th century, emerged out of ORANGE theology and values. "Unity" Centers and "Centers for Spiritual Living," for example, while culturally GREEN, teach ORANGE New Thought theology and interpret the Bible metaphysically.

Some Modern Christian influencers are the Jesus Seminar which has worked diligently to understand which words Jesus might have spoken. John Shelby Spong has written many books that deconstruct Biblical myths and challenge the church to reform its theology to be consistent with the Modern worldview. John Dominic Crosson suggests that Jesus not only taught in parables but that the entire story of Jesus might be a parable. Spiritual social action motivated by ORANGE values might focus on economic and educational efforts to advance a population's prosperity.

The GREEN vMeme

The GREEN vMeme has a Post-Modern, pluralistic perception of God. A person whose consciousness is centered in GREEN might fill in the blanks as follows: "God is an energetic benevolent presence. We are instruments of God's love."

Post-Modern, progressive, pluralistic consciousness sees a God who is the energy of Love, which translates into values of unity, inclusivity, and diversity. Marking a deliberate break from the BLUE "God of our fathers," and incorporating the individuality of the ORANGE Modern worldview, GREEN Post-Modern thinkers prefer to call themselves "spiritual, not religious." GREEN seeks wisdom in all religions and adds those beliefs and practices to its perception of God. There are no hierarchy levels, no respecter of status.

We noticed surprising stories of forgiveness in the Hebrew Bible, and some radical thoughts coming out of the Wisdom writings that were seeds of GREEN Post-Modern consciousness. If we take a look at the religious writings coming out of the first and second century CE, we can contrast the early story of the Tower of Babel, with its purple/RED jealous God, to the story of Pentecost (described by the Jewish followers of Jesus c. 33 CE). The miracle of Pentecost displays the GREEN perception of an inclusive, loving God that unites for the good of all. "All of them were filled with the Holy Spirit and began to speak in other languages, as the Spirit gave them ability . . . And at this sound, the crowd gathered and was bewildered, because each one heard them speaking in the native language of each" (Acts 2:4,6). We can also see hints of a GREEN cooperative living arrangement in the Christian book of Acts. (Acts 4:32-37).

The writers of the gospels report that Jesus expressed some pretty baffling (GREEN and 2nd Tier) ideas about money, belongings, and forgiveness. But the BLUE vMeme was still gaining momentum in the culture and would culminate in the creation of the institutional, orthodox synagogue and church. These hints of GREEN were just inconceivable to the people who tried to practice Jesus' teachings. They could only understand Jesus' parables and lessons from their red/BLUE worldview, so they created a monument (BLUE) about the enlightened man whose remarkable ideas came out of the 2nd Tier.

GREEN Progressive, Post-Modern spirituality seeks a mystical experience of God and practices awareness of the sacred.

Post-Moderns typically do not consider the Bible as the exclusive word of God since they choose to seek wisdom in writings from various cultures. GREEN theology, labeled "Progressive," tends to focus on the call for social justice, ecology, and economic reform based on the belief that God is Benevolence and all people deserve equal access to the bounty of this Earth. Progressive Christians, for example, focus primarily on the parts of the Bible that demonstrate Jesus' radical socio-economic and social justice teachings and on Jesus' prayer practice as a path to healing and wholeness.[60] GREEN perceives that God is a Being of Love who will restore health to the planet and believes that humans are the hands and feet of God's restorative project. People are motivated to passionate spiritual social action by this belief. And to be sure, the GREEN lifestyle is like a religion itself, which has been capitalized by ORANGE marketing.

GREEN's Faith-based social action's focus is on economic and environmental justice and radical compassion and often repurposes the ancient Hebrew prophets' call for justice to speak to the injustices created by Modern ORANGE. Marcus Borg was a leading Post-Modern (progressive) Christian influencer who read the Bible through the GREEN Post-Modern lens. He saw the Hebrew prophets' call to justice and equanimity as a pertinent message to 20th-century injustices.[61]

The Post-Modern GREEN worldview influences religion through interfaith celebrations, identifying a loving God who has preferential treatment for the poor and redefining religious action as social action demonstrated in justice reform, economic reform, and public protests.

GREEN spirituality swings back into anthropomorphizing God. In contrast to the heady abstract ORANGE concept of God, a person-centered in GREEN desires a relationship with the divine. God is often re-named "The Universe," which is highly personified in GREEN spiritual imagery. The Post-Modern God is both a masculine and feminine force within humankind, often addressed as 'Father-Mother God.' Everyone has access to the divine through inner work, and all paths to God are legitimate.

ORANGE Modern spiritual ideas clash with GREEN Post-Modern ones. One insists that God is *Principle, and* the other insists that God is *Love.* Jesus' disciple Mary went to the tomb to anoint Jesus' dead body and found him gone. The Post-Modern might initially react with despair to the concept that God is Principle, thinking, like Mary, "They've taken my Lord and I don't know where to find him."[62]

Second Tier YELLOW vMeme

Is God an impersonal Principle or is God an energy of Love? At the Second Tier, it's possible to see a compatible harmony between the two perspectives. Dr. Cady teaches,

> "There is no real reason why we, having come to recognize God as infinite substance, should be by this recognition deprived of the familiar fatherly companionship that in all ages has been so dear to the human heart. There is no necessity for us to separate God as substance and God as tender Father; no reason why we should not, and every reason why we should have both in one; they are one: God principle outside of us as unchangeable law, and God within us as tender, loving Father-Mother, who has compassion for our every sorrow. . . .. Every metaphysician reaches a place where God as cold principle alone will not suffice any more than in the past God as personality alone could wholly satisfy. At such times there will come but little comfort from the thought: 'This suffering comes as a result of my wrong thinking, but Principle takes no cognizance of it: I must work it out unaided and alone.' Just here we must have, and we do have, the motherhood of God, which is not cold Principle any more than your love for your child

is cold. I would not make God as Principle less, but God as individual more."[63]

Cady's ideas display the 2nd Tier integral worldview. As mentioned, one First-Tier stage cannot understand another that is two steps away on the Spiral. ORANGE would vehemently reject Cady's ideas. GREEN would be relieved. The goal is to be able to incorporate both into your perception of God. This is an integral practice.

The YELLOW Integral vMeme might fill in the blanks as follows: "God is the mastermind and master artist behind all ideas. I am the essence of God, therefore I am God.

YELLOW spiritual understanding is one of integration: all parts of the human experience are part of the whole, and each stage has aspects of its spirituality that provide a lasting contribution to the spiral."[64]

True to its name, the Integral vMeme recognizes and honors the wisdom contributed by shamans, prophets, messiahs, mystics, theologians, philosophers, scientists, and psychologists, and at the same time, realizes that each must personally and responsibly find their understanding and practice of good, truth, and beauty. YELLOW's desire for exploration of the spiritual joy of living leads them to eagerly maintain the meditation and self-awareness practices that brought them into integral thinking.

YELLOW seeks an individual understanding of the new world it has awakened to. It steps out of the community to explore, accumulate ideas, and assimilate a holistic understanding. It collects information with a passion. The percentage of the world population in the 2nd Tier is very small. Perhaps 1%. So eventually YELLOW can feel lonely: no one seems to be able to talk about the ideas they are entertaining. The internet serves as a way to connect with other 2nd Tier practitioners. Many evolutionary teachers agree that since the COVID pandemic, many more have moved into 2nd Tier consciousness. We will see how this affects society in the years to come.

The TURQUOISE v Meme

TURQUOISE is emerging simultaneously with YELLOW. The TURQUOISE vMeme might fill in the blanks as follows: "God is One. We are God."

The TURQUOISE worldview is known as a holistic consciousness. It perceives that the web of life is charged with spiritual energy and knows that this energy is the source of life. TURQUOISE spirituality has a strong focus on developing community with others who have awakened to the 2nd Tier experience of life.

Second Tier worldviews are capable of honoring all perspectives about ancient sacred scripture. The Bible is sacred and devotional, (PURPLE) it speaks with authority, (RED/BLUE) it is to be viewed with educated skepticism, (ORANGE) and it is a guide for radical compassionate living. (GREEN).

In this study, we noticed that the Bible portrays God and humankind in a relationship of conditional love. In first Tier consciousness, we tend to believe that God will love us only if we walk the righteous path. Or God will love us if we confess our sins and accept salvation. We extend this to our human relationships: people will love us if we please them in some way. In the 1st Tier consciousness, fear, lack, and competition are our dominant motivators. In 2nd Tier, we master the fear-based beliefs, and accept that love is unconditional. Jesus of Nazareth, who taught from a Second-Tier perspective, taught people to "Love your enemies, do good, and lend, expecting nothing in return." (Luke 6:35). The concept of unconditional love that Jesus taught was an impossible conceptual leap for the people of the Second Temple period in the first century CE, and many centuries following.

Practicing Integral Thinking

In evolutionary circles, we often hear the phrase "Wake up, Grow up, Clean up, Show up."[65] It's a guide that helps us remember that waking up is just the beginning of the discovery of the new world, the

Second Tier. We "grow up" by learning and gaining self-awareness. Just as we can use the Spiral Dynamics integral model to comprehend the ancient sacred texts and explain humankind's evolving perception of God, we can apply this model to our practice to grow into spiritual maturity or to "grow up."

We "clean up" by exposing our personality secrets (shadows and scars) to the light of loving truth. We can clean up in a variety of ways: through a talk with a spiritual mentor or director, therapy, spiritual retreats, group book studies in a confidential safe circle, vision quests, or other methods. We want to clean up to free ourselves from suffering (fear, attachment, resistance, unforgiveness). The result is the freedom to be whole, having removed the barriers that hid our radiance, we "show up" as the light of the world, an incarnation of the Oneness. Using the healthy and unhealthy characteristics of each stage listed below, we can conduct a courageous inventory of our consciousness. We can practice integral thinking by revisiting each vMeme and correlating each worldview to an aspect of our consciousness.

PURPLE vMeme

The "spiritual but not religious" population tends to glorify PURPLE, but it is a pre-rational worldview, and therefore carries with it a consciousness of fear, confusion, superstition, and helplessness. (We might wish we could be as imaginative as a three-year-old, but we wouldn't want to give up what the other stages of our lives have taught us.) When we do the work of "transcend and include", we can adopt PURPLE values into our post-Modern intellect.

Healthy PURPLE is active in the human consciousness when we sense a spiritual message in connection to natural phenomenon or when we are keenly aware of our intuition. It can show up in unhealthy ways when people directly correlate circumstances with the whim of the divine forces. For example, when Hurricane Katrina blasted New Orleans, some religious traditionalists, displaying the superstition of PURPLE, wondered aloud if God had sent the storm to clean up a sinful city.

Consider these healthy PURPLE characteristics through the lens of a Second-Tier holistic worldview.

- Do I recognize the value of family? The security of a group?
- Have I developed a conscious connection to nature?
- Am I comfortable doing self-expression through art and ritual?
- Do I recognize the feminine aspect of power? Spirituality?
- Am I tuned in to emotional nuances, Am I noticing intuitive information?

Consider these unhealthy PURPLE characteristics that you want to release:

- Do I detect fear-based thinking?
- Do I catch myself being exclusive of "others?"
- Am I resistant to adapting to innovation? New concepts?
- Am I willing to make room for the mystical in my busy mind?

RED vMeme

Many people tend to view RED as a selfish, undesirable stage. However, the RED worldview is an essential developmental step after PURPLE consciousness. Healthy RED spiritual practices can present as someone having the strength and courage to stand up to their superstitious fears or the victim consciousness of PURPLE. It shines through the person who dares to break away from strict ethnic lifestyle restrictions and set off to learn who they are. This spiritual warrior takes command of their attachments or addictions and boldly steps into "victory" consciousness.

Unhealthy RED religious practices display as the spiritual warrior looking to "slay dragons," or "defeat evil" by standing up for "the right thing." The person with those sentiments defines who is right and wrong, from the small aperture of their view of "the stupendous whole."

Consider these healthy RED practices to include in your holistic worldview.

- Can I take leadership? Am I willing to take risks?
- Can I express my opinion? Stand in my position? Set clear boundaries?
- Am I decisive; courageous? Am I able to take individual action? "I Am that I Am."
- Am I living from authentic spiritual strength, self-confidence, and strength of purpose?

Consider these unhealthy RED characteristics that you want to release.

- Do I notice myself resisting sharing power? Do I insist on having control?
- Do I feel emotionally challenged when someone disagrees with me or offers constructive criticism?
- Am I excessive about my reputation? (Do I watch how many "followers" I have?)
- Do I sometimes act before considering who might get hurt?
- Am I quick to use forceful assertive power to get what I want?

(Be aware that RED resistance can flare up when you're feeling burn-out. You feel like the world is a jungle. This would indicate a need to provide self-care and rest.) Consider your interactions with others in your personal and professional life. Do you declare powerful I Am statements that prepare you for your daily challenges? Are you living from the audacious powerful Self that you are?

BLUE vMeme

Consider these healthy BLUE practices to include in your holistic worldview.

- Do I respect principles and order; and practice neatness and cleanliness?
- Do I endeavor to do "what's right;" and consider ethics and societal norms before I act?
- Do I value fair laws and fair penalties; follow the law, the bylaws?
- Do I behave with honor and respect toward others?
- Do I value the use of myth to teach truisms?

Consider these unhealthy BLUE characteristics that we want to transcend as we evolve:

- Do I put tradition above progress?
- Am I unwilling to take risks? Am I resistant to the chaos of change?
- Am I inflexible and exclusionary of anyone who breaks the rules, or questions the norms?
- Do I catch myself thinking there is only one right way; seeing in "black and white," unable to perceive "grey areas?"
- Am I afraid of punishment for mistakes I make?
- Am I overly dependent on authority; Do I follow regulations blindly, without questioning their sensibility?

Where is your center of gravity on the Spiral? Imagine that you are standing on a huge model of the Spiral. You might find one foot, so to speak, in BLUE and another foot in ORANGE. Or you might see that one foot is in ORANGE and the other in GREEN. You might notice that you are rather BLUE in your religious life, but ORANGE in your professional life. You might be kind of GREEN in your parenting practices, or you might be experimenting with a cooperative living situation. This is not unusual. Just as societies are complex and stratified,[66] so are our worldviews. The integral practice is to notice your values and honor what is healthy, but release what is unhealthy, allowing yourself to expand into a true love of diversity and honest inclusiveness of divergent ideas.

ORANGE vMeme

Consider healthy ORANGE Modern practices that we want to include in a holistic worldview:

- Do I see that I am part of a global community?
- Do I enjoy self-improvement? Do I set goals and plan things out?
- Do I value science and rational thinking? Do I trust science?
- Do I make plans, act on promising possibilities, and initiate entrepreneurial projects?
- Do I perceive the divinity of the inner spiritual Self?
- Do I practice my ability to change my life experience by changing how I think?

Consider the unhealthy characteristics that we want to transcend as we mature:

- Must I win and do I believe that everyone else wants to win?
- Do I ignore or abuse Earth's resources, choosing without compassion?
- Do I sometimes get into unethical interactions; overwhelmed by competition and self-promotion?

The Modern ORANGE stage of development might lead a person out of the traditional BLUE church and into no church at all. Or they might feel drawn to a program church that offers prosperity teachings, intellectual stimulation, and programs for all ages. Considering New Thought teachings of the Law of Mind

Action and other Universal Principles, we can see that New Thought is centered in ORANGE. Unity's founders Charles and Myrtle Fillmore called the movement "Practical Christianity" because it applies Jesus' teachings as practical advice for living. This value indicates their Modern (ORANGE) worldview.

GREEN vMeme

Consider the healthy GREEN practices that you want to include in your holistic worldview:

- Do I honor equality for all? Do I value everyone's voice?
- Do I actively care about others' well-being? Do I act for the health of the planet?
- Do I process decisions with a balance of mind and heart?
- Am I dedicated to continuing my self-growth? Am I a steady spiritual practitioner?

Consider the unhealthy GREEN characteristics that we want to transcend as we mature:

- Do I get swayed by "group think?" Do I sometimes get caught up in conspiracy theories?
- Do I insist on collective problem-solving, distrusting hierarchical decision-making?
- Am I influenced by others' opinions; or overly concerned about fitting in?
- Am I focused on what I'm "against" rather than finding solutions?
- Do I sometimes feel like a victim in my efforts to establish justice and equal rights?
- Do I judge everybody else who isn't as progressive as me?

Popular GREEN spirituality like meditation, yoga, and spiritual book groups offer transformative experiences but many people go to classes without applying the practice toward transformation. When the peace activist and spiritual groupie becomes discontent with Post-Modern popular spirituality, the next step is to bring the concepts into a personal, responsible, and responsive worldview that integrates it all. This begins the momentous consciousness shift to the Second Tier of the Spiral.

At the top of the First Tier, we might assume that GREEN would seem most like an adult, but it is still fear-based, often blaming all the other vMemes for the economic, environmental, and cultural problems. GREEN's existential fear is for the ecological and economic health of the planet: fear of possible extinction of the world as we know it. When we consider what we want to include as we transcend into the 2nd Tier, we notice that GREEN's values are strongly passionate and rooted in urgent fear.

To adopt a holistic worldview, consider these additional questions:

- Am I willing to realize that saving the world is not up to me?
- Do I understand that saving the world might not look like I thought it should?
- Am I ready to stop judging everything?
- Can I flex and flow with change?
- Am I willing to introduce spiritual practices or create thoughts that integrate healthy aspects from every level of the Spiral?
- What practices can I do that will help me release the habitual thought patterns that stand in the way of understanding "the stupendous whole?"

The biggest shift we make when we enter YELLOW (2nd Tier) is that we release fear. We will include GREEN's values but release the fear and the urgency. A big indicator that you are exiting GREEN and thinking like YELLOW is that you are less fearful of the doomsday possibilities. Instead, you feel hopeful that the chaos you're witnessing is the start of the momentous shift that Clare Graves prophesied.

"Humans must prepare for a momentous leap…The present moment finds our society attempting to negotiate the most difficult, but at the same time the most exciting transition humans have faced to date. It is not merely a transition to a new level of existence but the start of a new 'movement' in the symphony of human history." Clare Graves[67]

Processing This Chapter:

(The numbers do not indicate suggested order or importance.)

1. After this study of the Hebrew Scriptures through an Evolutionary lens, how would you now describe to a friend how the Bible could be seen as the story of the development of human consciousness?

2. As with all universal truth, the teachings of the Bible continue to inform consciousness, at whatever level these truth statements are understood. Consider how different worldviews might understand Proverbs 3:6: "Trust in the Lord with all your heart and lean not unto your own understanding. In all thy ways acknowledge Him and He will direct thy paths." This is from the King James Version which is written from a BLUE perspective. This translation defines a masculine God that expects full devotion. It expects devotees to follow, not act on their own ideas. ORANGE might paraphrase it this way: "Trust the Laws of the Universe and lean not on human understanding. In all aspects of your life work with Principle and It will illumine your decisions." Or it might say, "Trust the "I Am" within…" These paraphrases remove the authoritarian BLUE personified God. It depicts God as Principle and emphasizes individual responsibility. Continue the process with GREEN, YELLOW, and TURQUOISE.

3. The Absolute Truths that Jesus taught can be understood in every worldview. Consider how each vMeme might interpret the teaching "Seek ye first the kingdom of God." First, consider the PURPLE tribal chief; then the RED religious fanatic; the BLUE prophet; the ORANGE metaphysician; the GREEN social activist. How would a Second-Tier practitioner read from this phrase? (Read and consider the surrounding context of the phrase from Matthew 6: 25-34). Or reflect in the same way on this teaching of Jesus: "If you continue in my word, you are truly my disciples; and you will know the truth, and the truth will make you free." (John 8: 31-32)

If you are ready to explore the 2nd Tier a little further,

1. For comprehensive details about every ᵛMeme including those beyond TURQUOISE, visit SDiNL Spiral Dynamics Integral Netherlands
www. spiraldynamicsintegral.nl/en/valuesystems

2. Subscribe to the YouTube channel *Shores of Infinity*. Find the playlist called "Spiral Dynamics" on the home page of *Wake Up!* These videos are produced by Christian Weidl, but you won't easily find his name. In the summer of 2020, during the shutdown because of the pandemic, Chris produced many videos about Spiral Dynamics, including topics of exit-GREEN, YELLOW, TURQUOISE, CORAL, AND TEAL. https://www.youtube.com/c/Wakeupcrashingontheshoresof8/featured

3. Subscribe to *The Daily Evolver* by Jeff Salzman. He speaks Ken Wilber language, but it ties in closely with Spiral Dynamics, and he offers commentary about the world from a Post-Progressive (exit-GREEN) perspective. Available on YouTube and podcast. https://www.youtube.com/c/DailyEvolver

4. Check out the YouTube channel *Actualized.org*. Leo Gura has 11 videos on his playlist called Developmental Psychology and Spiral Dynamics. https://www.youtube.com/c/ActualizedOrg

Appendix

The Spiral Dynamics Model

A model for understanding the dynamic forces at work in the process of human development.

Part One. Evolution

Charles Darwin published his theory of evolution in 1859 and within a dozen years, the scientific community and most of the educated public had widely accepted evolution as a fact. By the end of the 19th century, evolutionary imagery had made its appearance through science, literature, and politics and there was no serious scientific opposition to the basic evolutionary theory of biological evolution. Observations on the evolution of human consciousness by Henri Bergson, Jean Gebser, Abraham Maslow, and Clare Graves contributed to this field of knowledge, and by the mid-twentieth century, an "integral" theory of evolution emerged.

The cosmos, the organism, and the consciousness has been continuously evolving since the beginning of our universe. Integral consciousness acknowledges, and values all our previous value systems, creating a worldview that is fully integrated. Integral theory recognizes that evolution takes place in the development of culture and consciousness (the interior), as well as in the body and structures (the exterior). To integrate all the stages of consciousness, practice integral thinking. Those who can stretch into an integral worldview will notice they can relate without judgment to other worldviews.

Current influential thinkers of the Integral evolutionary theory include Don Beck of Spiral Dynamics, Ken Wilber, Steve McIntosh, Alan Combs, Carter Phipps, and others.

Spiral Dynamics does not label 'types' of people. It provides insight into people's behavior based on what people value in a certain context at a certain level of awareness. The model draws parallels between collective consciousness and individual psycho/social development. It concurs with the latest findings of both organizational theorists and neurobiology. Knowledge about Spiral Dynamics is extremely valuable for understanding the versatile needs (values and motives) of individuals, teams, organizations, and society and for aligning them most optimally and effectively.

People of Spiral Dynamics

Clare W. Graves, Ph.D., began laying the groundwork for the theory behind Spiral Dynamics in the 1950s. He specialized in applied theories of personality. In his teaching and research, at Union College, New York, he sought a comprehensive theory that could answer his basic question, "What is healthy, mature, human behavior?"

Integrating the work of others who had developed several foundational theories, Clare Graves developed several theories toward a multi-disciplinary understanding of human growth and development. Dr. Graves led a clinical study to explore and answer his research questions. Interviewing thousands of study participants over 30 years, Dr. Graves integrated themes from psychology, anthropology, sociology, the neurosciences, philosophy, and the arts. His collected data presented

Evolutionary Thinkers behind Spiral Dynamics:
Bergson: 1859-1941
Teilhard: 1881-1955
Jung: 1875-1961
Maslow: 1908-1970
Gebser: 1905-1973
Graves: 1914-1986
Beck: 1937-2022

comprehensive reasons behind the shifting nature of human

worldviews. He drafted a multi-dimensional spiral shape to develop a model for understanding the evolutionary transformation of human values and cultures.

Graves' conclusion of his research was that people's attitudes and behaviors arise from cultural value and belief systems and their own bio-psycho-social development.

"... the psychology of the mature human being is an unfolding, emergent, oscillating, spiraling process, marked by progressive subordination of older, lower-order behavior systems to newer, higher-order systems as man's existential problems change."

Don Beck and Chris Cowan carried the torch of Clare Graves' research and coined the term Spiral Dynamics in the 1990s. Their book *Spiral Dynamics and the Evolution of Consciousness* is the classic primer on the subject. Beck used the model in many disciplines such as business, government, community organization, sports, rehabilitation, and recovery programs. Dr. Beck developed, implemented, and taught Spiral Dynamics for more than three decades.

The Spiral Icon

The spiral is the perfect icon for the evolution of consciousness. It is an ancient symbol valued on every populated continent. At burial sites across the globe, it represents the "life-death-rebirth" cycle and our inner and outer journey to God and the Self. Carl Jung explained that spirals represent a journey into the collective unconscious and then back into the world renewed with a greater psychological understanding of who we are and why we are here.

The spiral shape indicates that we come "back around" as we journey through our stages of faith. As we mature, we reconcile with who we were or what we did in the past. Over the decades as we revisit our past, we can see it from an evolved worldview, a more mature level of consciousness.

Charles Fillmore, a co-founder of the Unity movement, saw the significance of the spiral in the study of consciousness:

> "In his evolution man has apparently always moved in cycles, but each time he comes again to his starting place he seems to be a little in advance of his former state."[68]

> "He who studies Mind may know how to "discern the signs of the times." He becomes familiar with certain underlying principles, and he recognizes them in their different masks in "the whirligig of time." Under the veil of historical symbology, the Scriptures portray the movements of Mind in its different cycles of progress. These cycles repeat themselves over and over again, but each time on a higher plane. Thus the sphere or circle is a type of the complete Mind, but in manifestation, the circles are piled one on top of another in an infinite spiral." [69]

The spiral journey of human development described in Spiral Dynamics begins with a narrow point of focus, then expands with each turn and increases in breadth, diversity, and complexity. As individual and collective consciousness evolves, the worldview expands into increasingly wider circles of more complexity (more diversity, more variety, more chaos, more demands…). These circles expand to meet changed life conditions, producing new ideas, new values, and new norms to deal effectively with these new life conditions. In the evolutionary progression, at any time or place on the planet, we can find people who represent every stage of the Spiral.

SPIRAL TERMS AND CONCEPTS

We will devote Part Two of this Appendix to each vMeme of the Spiral, but first, some terms and concepts used by Spiral Dynamics about the evolution of consciousness:

Consciousness: Consciousness in an individual and the collective is "experiential" awareness consisting of feelings, thoughts, intentions, and our sense of identity, the subjective presence of every living person.

vMeme: vMemes are also called Value Systems, World Views, Stages, Structures, Waves of Consciousness, Levels of Consciousness, Frames of Reference, Paradigms, and Phases in Conscious Development. *vMeme* emphasizes the *values* associated with worldviews: how people think and why they adopt the values they do. Each new worldview introduces a set of values in response to current life conditions and societal problems. A vMeme is a perspective from which you see your world. It's your paradigm: the lenses through which you view the world. Our worldview acts like a filter or a magnet: we notice and accept information that is in alignment with our existing worldview, and we avoid or reject the ideas that aren't. When we confront a life event that challenges that worldview, our paradigm adjusts. Individual paradigm shifts subtly influence the collective consciousness, and vice versa, the collective consciousness influences individuals.

Value systems are interior, and they should not be confused with behavior, which is exterior. A paradigm shift is interior and will need time to manifest in the exterior: our behavior and practices. No one sees 100% from only one worldview. They will have their feet in different vMemes of the spiral depending on if they're thinking about religion, politics, economics, education, family systems, etc. It follows that a shift in worldview is not a sure step into the next vMeme. As individuals and as a collective society, we will always be acting, reacting, and pondering life through different lenses simultaneously.

The Spiral Dynamics model depicts stages of psychological, social, and spiritual evolution that are fluid. You might imagine it as a "wave." We move into the next level incrementally, often unconsciously. We adjust our focus depending on our life conditions. We stretch into new values until they become our core values. As we evolve, we will notice that we seem to have one foot in one level and the other foot in the next level. Similarly, collective consciousness shifts at a grass-roots level: one thinker at a time. Eventually, the new value system has momentum and becomes the predominant one.

One vMeme is not "better" or "worse" than a prior vMeme. Each successive stage indicates a more expansive outlook or worldview, and each provides more influence and more efficiency, but it does not imply that one is "better" than another. This makes perfect sense if you compare it to comparing two children, a 5-year-old, and a 10-year-old. You would not declare that the 10-year-old is "better" because he is more capable and has a more expanded worldview than the 5-year-old.)

Transcend and Include

Culturally, humans don't "throw the baby out with the bathwater." We don't dispose of every aspect of one worldview when we evolve into the next. We carry them forward, integrating aspects of earlier beliefs and views into the next and the next. Each new worldview is increasingly complex and expansive.

"Transcend and include" is a common phrase when we speak of evolution. Each vMeme has healthy and unhealthy characteristics. As humans mature individually and collectively, they "transcend" (or leave behind) the characteristics that are unhealthy and "include" (carry forward) those that are healthy.

The Spiral Dynamics model allows the accumulation of good aspects of previous stages (vMemes) that continue to serve well in current life conditions.

> "One of the chief beauties of the spiral as an imaginative conception is that it is always growing, yet never covering the same ground, so that it is not merely an explanation of the past, but it is also a prophecy of the future; and while it defines and illuminates what has already happened, it is also leading constantly to new discoveries."[70]

In both personal and collective evolution, we must work through unhealthy or unfinished areas of each vMeme before we expect to be healthy in the next level. Sometimes Life Conditions thrust people into stages that they are not yet ready for. They might completely skip a stage of development. If they don't work through these stages, they'll get a chance to loop back around later in life as they begin the search for emotional and spiritual maturity.

The Push and the Pull

The Push: Life Conditions: When a change occurs, it's because of both a "push" and a "pull." The push is our drive to survive and prosper. Any aspect of the environment that affects consciousness is called a "Life Condition." Changes in Life conditions put great pressure on consciousness to change in order to adapt and find solutions to survive the new life conditions. If the current worldview or structure cannot competently address emerging life conditions, a new worldview emerges to address the new conditions. New values will rise, gradually, from the grassroots, in response to new life conditions.

> *"You never change things by fighting the existing reality. To change something, build a new model that makes the existing model obsolete."* – R. Buckminster Fuller

> *"The structures of the internal universe are subtle and complex. They are better compared to ocean currents than to architecture. Each stage of consciousness is a way of making meaning of the worldview that arises from a set of problematic life conditions and their corresponding solutions."* – *Richard Dawkins*[71]

The Pull: Evolutionary Impulse

The pull is the innate impulse of all life forms to grow and expand. Observing the long-term evolution of human consciousness, we can agree that humankind's consciousness has risen toward higher ideals. Even if we see way too much violence and greed going on, over the long haul, we have continuously created a more complex and expansive consciousness. This innate drive toward expansion arises from the attracting power of the hopeful, fresh potential of new stages: new Truth, new

Beauty, new Ideals. This "pull" is what we might call the evolutionary impulse or divine discontent, the "Omega Point", or Love or God. The push and the pull are the creative aspect of our consciousness, the human dilemma: the value of self-preservation in a dance with the innate desire for self-transcendence.

Transformational Dilemma

Humans will get settled into a worldview and remain there for as long as it serves their needs. But when changing life conditions present new challenges and the current dominant vMeme doesn't address them, a new worldview emerges with a new outlook to address the problems. There will be tension during this time, as one experiences chaos and change, releasing old paradigms and adapting to new ways to perceive the world. At any given time on the planet, one or another or all of the global communities experience Transformational Dilemmas, as the Life Conditions force innovative societal reforms. We can use this information to become aware and anticipate the needs that will arise as a community moves from one vMeme to the next in the model. They will need certain guidance and insights, depending on which two vMemes are in play.

Two Tiers

The First Tier of the Spiral consists of six ᵛMemes. Each are considered "subsistence" levels, with a focus on survival, self-identity, and "doing." In the First Tier, when one is in a certain worldview or ᵛMeme, they can't understand or empathize with other worldviews. One's current worldview is the only one that makes sense, and all the others are "wrong" or "evil." This inability to value other points of view is characteristic of every ᵛMeme in the 1ˢᵗ Tier.

Movement into the Second Tier is a "giant leap" in consciousness, with a focus on "being." In the 2ⁿᵈ Tier, people synthesize the wisdom and lessons of all prior stages. They can empathize and have compassion for each level without judgment. One might say that the First Tier is about "making a living;" and the 2ⁿᵈ Tier is about "making a life." More stages of the 2ⁿᵈ Tier are being identified and clarified as we evolve collectively and individually.

Harbingers of Change, Seeds of Consciousness.

Every level has luminaries who can conceptualize ideas that aren't within the current worldview and attempt to suggest them to their contemporaries. These 'harbingers of change' have been persecuted by people of less vision and with vested interests in preserving the status quo. These far-sighted visionaries do, however, plant 'seeds of consciousness' that eventually are appreciated and instituted. Our visionaries, mystics, prophets, and messiah-figures are 'harbingers of change.'

Pierre Teilhard do Chardin (1881-1955), (pronounce his name like the French: *tay are duh shar-dan*), Jesuit priest and paleontologist was a Harbinger of Change whose evolutionary ideas were hushed by the Roman Catholic church. In 1925, he chose to stop publishing his ideas in order to remain a priest. It was not until the 1960's that his works were published and defended by scholars.

Teilhard had a mystical insight" *"Love is the scared reserve of energy , the blood of spiritual evolution,"* Reflecting on that inspired phrase, he wrote, *"The word 'evolution' haunted my thoughts like a tune, which to me was like an unsatisfied hunger, like a promise held out to me, like a summons to be answered."* He posited that we are moving toward an 'Omega Point,' the point to which all beings long to return, and its drawing power is Love, which he considered synonymous with 'God.'

Teilhard was not familiar with Spiral Dynamics, but he understood the concept. His inspirational teachings inform the spiritual aspect of integral theory of conscious evolution.

The Colors of the Spial

The colors are for ease of recall and communication about the levels. They are not related to chakras nor spectrum colors but are related to the life conditions that correspond with each level. Beige: the color of the savannah where humans originated; PURPLE: a color associated with magic; RED: violence; BLUE: loyalty; ORANGE: vivid action; GREEN: ecology. (Search engine: Spiral Dynamics "images")

"I" or "We"

Individually and collectively, human worldviews swing like a pendulum between "I" and "We." We oscillate between autonomous thinking (individual, self-determination) and cooperative thinking, (collective, self-sacrifice). The colors identify this swing: alternative warm colors BEIGE, RED, ORANGE, YELLOW, CORAL convey the "I" orientation. Cool colors PURPLE, BLUE, GREEN, TURQUOISE convey the "We" orientation. Typically, when a cooperative ᵛMeme emerges, it vehemently denounces and condemns the previous Individualistic ᵛMeme, demanding social reform. When the "I" Meme emerges, it challenges the previous paradigm to adjust to change and innovation.

Moving sequentially

We should not attempt to skip over any stage. Each one is essential to the health and wellbeing of development. This applies to businesses, government, and organizations, and is particularly important to remember if you are trying to help an organization or individual improve their life situation. For example, if they are in a RED consciousness, their natural next stage is BLUE. The values of BLUE such as cooperation, loyalty, and justice will address their concerns and open a way for them to resolve their issues. Skipping a level in one's individual development is also not recommended. Many try to "be good" throughout their childhood and then find themselves having a mid-life rebellious stage, which allows them to experience the rebellious RED individuality that they ignored earlier in life.

"We are quite naturally impatient in everything to reach the end without delay. We should like to skip the intermediate

stages. We are impatient of being on the way to something unknown, something new. And yet it is the law of all progress that it is made by passing through stages of instability... your ideas mature gradually let them grow, let them shape themselves, without undue haste. Don't try to force them on ...Only God could say what this new spirit gradually forming within you will be. ...accept the anxiety of feeling yourself in suspense and incomplete." Pierre Teilhard de Chardin[72]

Dialectical and Expanding

As the Spiral develops, we can see the Hegelian dialectic pattern of thesis, antithesis, and synthesis. The current stage serves its purpose, and the status quo is acceptable. (thesis) But it becomes corrupt and creates problematic social or economic conditions (antithesis) The status quo cannot solve the problems it has created. The next wave of consciousness emerges in response, and each displays greater degrees of sophistication and complexity in its response. (synthesis)

Never-Ending

Clare Graves saw human evolution as a "Never Ending Upward Quest," meaning that we have an unlimited creative ability to adapt and become something even more expansive, more creative. Looking at the model as a whole system, we see that this evolution of consciousness is limited only by our capacity to expand and evolve our thinking. Although we can become discouraged when sometimes society seems to be regressing, the Spiral shows us that things are improving! As the Spiral unfolds, we see an increase in values such as behavioral freedom, cognitive complexity, tolerance of ambiguity, distance from own beliefs, and creative novelty. We see a decrease in authoritarianism, rigidity, polarization, absolutism, exclusivity, and egocentrism.

Accelerating

History has recorded the approximate length of time humankind has spent in each 'Meme before moving on to the next level. The time spent in each stage is radically reduced with each step forward; 215,000 years in BEIGE to 7,000 years in RED to 400 years in ORANGE. The pace of cultural evolution is drastically speeding up, and multiple voices representing contemporaneous worldviews are interacting and clashing, causing the keen sense of the chaos we are experiencing today.

Part Two Description of the vMemes

Tier One

We begin our study at the beginning of human consciousness in BEIGE, which indicates the dawning of the human species, and the infancy stage of personal human development.

BEIGE vMeme: Survival; Instinctive, Archaic
"Do what I must to survive."

Our ancestors invested millions of years in developing their physical bodies and brains. At the earliest stage of homo sapiens, we focused all our energy on survival: food, warmth, and sexual instincts. "Instinctive BEIGE" can be considered the first link in the "Great Chain of Being." The BEIGE vMeme emerged about 250,000 and continued as the only worldview until about 35,000 years ago. This primarily instinctual consciousness is represented by the Neanderthal or Archaic Homo Sapiens; the Semi-stone age: Clans; Hunter/Gather. BEIGE is Individualistic and focused solely on survival.

> *"Dawn Man began his career immersed in the subconscious*
> *realms of nature and body, of vegetable and animal, and*

initially 'experienced' himself as indistinguishable from the world that had already evolved to that point"[73]

This is an extremely limited, non-reflective worldview, not unlike those of animals. Cognitive science considers this stage of human brain activity to be 95% unconscious, with almost no reflective thinking. Over the thousands of generations, biological evolution advanced: physical skills, memory, and psychic abilities gradually developed. Our ancient ancestors (and all of us as infants) lacked the physiological ability to articulate specific sounds, so language was limited to crude verbal cues and primitive sign language.

BEIGE Survival consciousness correlates to human development from 0-18 months. A human newborn is focused on specific survival needs. The eyes, the brain, and other organs are still developing. Gradually, the senses become keener, and the child explores the world with all their senses. Nuclear family identity develops.

Today, we see BEIGE in some adults, such as those who are dealing with mental illness, dementia, and chronic homelessness, as well as (temporarily) in refugees or disaster victims.

Transcend and Include

As we move through the stages, we include the values, norms, and behaviors that worked well for us and are still valued. We transcend those that no longer serve us or have become corrupt.

BEIGE characteristics that are included in the next level:

- Physical strength and quickness;
- Instinctive,
- Telepathic connection to nature;
- Sharpened senses;
- Attentive to rearing the young.
- BEIGE characteristics that we transcended as we evolved:
- inadequate language skills;

- no reflective thinking;
- preoccupied with survival.

Life Conditions and Transformational Dilemma

Further biological evolution of the voice box and corresponding neural networks allowed the faculty of speech, a major impetus for progress.

The Transformational Dilemma of Beige is that daily survival is exhausting. With the dawn of language and the growth of population, a natural shift, while including the need for survival, was to gather into a larger, organized tribe. The challenge for BEIGE was to learn to cooperate with a larger group.

PURPLE vMeme: Mystical; Magical; Tribal
"Keep the spirits happy and the tribe safe and warm."

About 40,000 years ago, after thousands of generations of survival and brain development, the PURPLE consciousness emerged. These ancestors are known as Homo Sapiens Cro-Magnon. This worldview was the predominant one for about 32,000 years and corresponds with the Paleolithic Age.

Speech stimulated the development of new mental and technical skills and enhanced imagination and intuition and enabled accumulated knowledge to be passed on from generation to generation. With language, our ancestors also developed conscious awareness. They became reflective. Still, the tribe functioned as one unit, not individuals, not distinguishable from their natural surroundings. They did, however, understand that "others" were not to be trusted. The PURPLE worldview has a strong sense of "us" and "them."

The PURPLE worldview is a "We" group-think tribal collective consciousness. Cooperation brought safety, a safe haven, and freedom to think beyond mere survival. As a tribe, our ancestors could hunt large game, which they had not been able to defeat alone. They refined techniques for tool and weapon-crafting and designed and built shelters.

> "The Cro-Magnons were inspiring and fascinating companions during the second mile of our evolutionary journey. They showed us so much about how the Spirit manifests itself in us, how humans can reflect upon their destiny, create beauty in all forms, love and create a compassionate society, and live in harmony with their fellow creatures and with nature." [74]

Jean Auel's *The Clan of the Cave Bear* provides a sense of the tribal group-think, the emphasis on ritual and unspoken cultural expectations, and the mystical interpretation of the world of PURPLE. The tribe's safety concern was often dictated by imagination and magical thinking. Spirits cause phases of the moon, changes in the wind, lightning, thunder, volcano, and earthquake. The tribe believed that they must not break from "the memories" so that the spirits wouldn't be angry. This fear compelled rituals including the sacrifice of animals and people to please the spirits and protect themselves. Sacrifice is indicative of PURPLE ᵛMeme, and the practice would continue into the next.

PURPLE is demonstrated in psychological human development from 1-3 years. By the 18th month, the toddler understands language and begins to speak. He displays curiosity and imagination. This worldview is the collective "we." Like the PURPLE consciousness of our ancestors, toddlers are subsumed into the family group. The very young human does not understand science and reason, so they will engage in magical imagination to explain phenomena. They engage in creative play, and joyful rituals, celebrate happiness with their entire body and bring love to their tribe. They often communicate in a crude language understood only by the immediate family, their tribe.

In contemporary society, PURPLE is vibrant in ethnic extended families, indigenous communities, religious cults, clan warfare, ancient grudges, use of folk remedies. It is present in the religious practices of sacraments, rituals, incense-burning, and mantras spoken in and unfamiliar language by priests in flowing robes. PURPLE is integrated into today's Post-Modern spirituality, (drumming, shamanism, natural remedies, vision-quests).

Spiral Dynamics PURPLE "KinSpirits" correlates with Gebser and Fowler's "Magic Intuitive-Projective." It corresponds with Wilber's "MAGENTA, Tribal."

We see purple/RED consciousness in the J & E writers of the Bible. We will study this worldview's perception of God in Chapters 4 and 5.

Characteristics/Values:

- "We" Self-Sacrifice "KinSpirits"
- KinSpirits: blood relationships & mysticism in a magical and scary world.
- Thinking is animistic; structures are tribal; processes are circular.
- tribal identity, "us vs them"
- Intuitive, attuned to nature and nuances.
- Obey the spirits and mystical signs.
- Show allegiance to the tribe and the elders; no individual thinking.
- Unspoken, uncompromising rules of conduct secure the clan's safety.
- Rituals, traditions, symbols, guardian angels, voodoo-curses, blood oaths, lucky charms, superstitions, and athletic team bonding.
- The ancient cave paintings and big-breasted goddess icons come out of this era.

Transcend and Include:

PURPLE characteristics that are included in next level:

- Security in numbers;
- Attention to the mysteries of life;
- Connection with nature;
- Read emotional nuances;
- Express through art and ritual;
- Recognize feminine power;
- Intuition;
- Imagination and fantasy.

Unhealthy PURPLE characteristics that we transcend:

- Fear-based thinking;
- Limitations upon self-expression;
- Slow to adapt;
- "Us vs. them" attitude.

Life Conditions and the Transformational Dilemma

The ancient Great Flood stories convey the life conditions on the globe when PURPLE was the dominant level of consciousness. The temperature of the earth rose, and mile-high ice masses melted. Sea levels rose 600 feet, flooding all coastal settlements. The waters of the Mediterranean Sea and the Black Sea breached the land with a force 200 times greater than Niagara Falls, inundating fishing villages and forming the present-day Bosporus Strait.

With warmer temperatures, plant and animal life flourished, and our ancestor's focus turned toward agriculture as a whole new way of survival. They grew wheat and barley. They bred sheep, goats, pigs, and cows for milk, wool, meat, and hides. Agriculture brought tribal security of survival, and with that basic need met, consciousness reached for more expansion. Independent thinkers began to emerge, and a desire for autonomy, self-expression, and power created tension in the PURPLE tribe. The Transformational Dilemma of Purple is that the environmental changes sparked a pull toward individuality and venturing outward. There was more opportunity "out there," and a greater chance of acquiring better resources by rising to power. Individuality would come from those who were courageous enough to buck the tribal system and venture into autonomy.

Tribal Movement around the globe during this period: (BCE)	
40,000	Glaciers cover N. Hemisphere
35,000	Migration across Bering Strait into N America
30,000	Inhabit Australia, Entered Europe. Neanderthals die out.
25,000	Cave Paintings: France, Spain; Goddess Icons: Europe, Egypt
15,000	N Africa was fertile and wet (until 10,000 BCE)
10,000	Middle East was fertile and moist (until 10,000 BCE)
9,000	Humans build walls to enclose Jericho

RED vMeme: Warrior; Egocentric

"Be what you are and do what you want, regardless."

RED vMeme emerged around 10,000 BCE and was predominant until around 3000 BCE. It is an Individualistic worldview.

RED consciousness is profoundly more advanced than PURPLE. At this stage, our ancestor's brain functions dramatically increased their ability to exercise will and assert the self. Hence this level of consciousness is called 'egocentric'. It was an era of great accomplishment because they also developed analytic and organizing skills.

The "cradles of civilization," Mesopotamia and Egypt are the results of RED consciousness. These empires dominated cultural, political, economic, and religious spheres for thousands of years, (long before the Bible was written.) As healthy RED civilizations, they farmed year-round, used a potter's wheel, had a centralized government with written laws, and developed medicine, astronomy, mathematics, and economic and civil structures. Copper and metal combined provided the ability to create effective weapons and tools, artwork, and buildings. Egypt, which had been in power in the region for many centuries already, began building pyramids circa 2550 BCE. Egypt controlled all the land on the eastern shore of the Mediterranean Sea, and everyone in that region was a vassal to the Pharaoh, until the collapse of the Bronze Age circa 1250 BCE.

RED awakened a breed of warrior and braggadocious myths: heroic deeds, vanquished enemies, and performing impossible physical feats. Reverence for the Earth mother turned to contests with her.

We see purple/RED consciousness in the J& E writers of the Bible. Awareness of the Israelites' identity as a "people," corresponds with the dawn of the Bronze Age, circa 3000 BCE. From the Spiral Dynamics perspective, we can infer that the Israelite identity emerged in purple/RED worldview.

RED Characteristics/Values

- "I" Individualistic: Power of Self, "PowerGods"
- Might makes right; Survive through might; dominate; exploitive independence
- Exploit unskilled, uneducated; does not honor others
- Impulsive: does not think of consequences nor danger; wants gratification now!
- Strict division of have's and have not's: run by elites
- Motivated by heroes & conquest

RED is demonstrated in psychological human development from 3 -6 years and in teenage years. After the toddler stage, the child asserts their own will, is often contrary, has no impulse control, and sometimes does things we would consider "cruel" or "unacceptable." RED egocentrism, although not fun for the parent, is a normal and necessary part of personality development. This egocentrism develops further in the teenage years when one is self-absorbed, harsh, insistent, impatient, and impulsive. RED's violence and turmoil serve as a "birth trauma" -- a fiery ordeal through which a developing civilization (and individual) must pass.

Today's RED shows up in street gangs, grass-roots militia

groups, soldiers of fortune, tribal warfare, terrorists, dictators, mafia, criminals, and fictional villains. RED voices express even in today's more "evolved" vMemes. Heavy Metal and Rap music genres convey the voice of the RED rebellious angry attitude in the middle of a Post-Modern worldview. RED is often misunderstood: being angry doesn't mean that you are RED. Every stage gets angry. It's why and what you'll do about the anger that displays your value meme.

Spiral Dynamics RED "PowerGods" correlates with Maslow's "Safety Needs" and Wilber's "RED Egocentric." We will study this worldview's perception of God in Chapter 5.

RED Transcend and Include

Characteristics to integrate into the next level:

- Ability to take individual action;
- Swift response to emergencies;
- Courage to take risks;
- Assertion of strong ego;
- Assertion of leadership;
- Aggressive and competitive;
- Expects rewards for building skills;
- Recognition of masculine power;
- Dedication to solving problems: internal & external;
- Sets clear boundaries and indicates urgency;
- Encourages expression of one's own opinion[75]

Unhealthy RED characteristics to transcend:

- Resists sharing power, and control;
- Acts regardless of who is hurt;
- Extreme negative emotions when thwarted;
- Reputation is more important than life;
- Overemphasis on masculine power.

Life Conditions and Transformational Dilemma

When the current vMeme has served its good purpose, it loses its effectiveness and cannot solve the problems it created. The RED value system of the Bronze Age had accomplished tremendous advances in technology and societal structure. But RED's egocentric selfishness and pride resulted in the exploitative rule of the few over the many. Strength had become so important that bloodshed had become a constant threat. Competition and harsh cruelty had produced an oppressive elite and a suffering victim populous. It had produced widows and fatherless children. To ensure the future of society the society needed to enforce cooperation.

About 6000 years ago, as populations increased, it became apparent that constant battles and warfare could not address the emerging society's needs. A new consciousness was required for reform to occur. The pendulum began its swing back to collective thinking and self-sacrifice for the good of the whole.

The Transformational Dilemma of Red is that impulsive, short-term thinking is disastrous in the long-run. It backfires, unintentionally hurting the organism and those close to it, threatening society's survival.

Tech and Art Developments during this period (BCE):

8000	Neolithic Age: Indigenous people, headed by big-chief
7000	Brick developed
6000	Necklaces made of cowrie shells
5000	Looms, weaving; Trade of obsidian, flint
3200	Earliest writing: Cuneiform, Pictorial

BLUE: Authoritarian, Purposeful, Traditional

"Life has meaning, direction, and purpose, with predetermined outcomes."

BLUE Authoritative Consciousness emerged in the "fertile crescent" of the Tigris and Euphrates rivers approximately 4000 BCE and was the predominant consciousness through around **1300 CE**. It emerged after the apocalyptic, disorganized and violent times following Egypt's collapse. By about 1000 BCE, BLUE values were evident in the Middle East.

BLUE corresponds with the Axial Age. The consciousness

163

pivoted from self-indulgence and violence to self-sacrifice and discipline. This was a time when all over the world, great philosophers and teachers were introducing parallel concepts, beliefs, and new social, moral, and ethical codes of conduct. Across the globe, as the BLUE worldview gained predominance the major religions formed, providing a quantum leap forward to advance new ways to live fruitfully and meaningfully.

BLUE is a "We" mindset that sacrifices self for the good of the whole. Order, discipline, meaning, and purpose were the new values. Absolute rules were established. Myth-making arose, with heroes exemplifying virtues, and with gods that would punish disobedience to the law and order. A wrathful God with absolute power could send warlords and soldiers-of-fortune to Hell or Heaven. These stories called the people to repent and conform for the greater good.

RED and PURPLE have a tribal outlook, but BLUE worldview has a national identity. Authoritarian BLUE's establishment of law and order, structure, allegiance, conformity, tradition, heritage, family, and obedience produced an era of great expansion, security, predictability, clear communication, and authoritarian decision-making.

BLUE Characteristics/Values:

- "We" Group-identity: "TruthForce"
- Find purpose, bring order, and future security;
- Absolute Truth; concrete-literal thinking;
- Fundamentalism, Fascism, Extremism;
- Self-sacrifice for a higher cause; Discipline;
- Responsibility; duty, obedience, honor;
- Law and order; Fair justice and mercy;
- Control through guilt; obedience to the rules; penalties for disobedience;
- Authoritarian; hierarchy, purpose, and patriotism;
- Life has direction and purpose under the control of ultimate truth.

We see BLUE consciousness in the P&D writers and the Prophets of the Bible. Most of the Bible is written from the BLUE worldview. They emphasized morality with the Ten Commandments. They wrote detailed cultic laws about food, clothing, and feasts. Their eloquent verbiage shows attention to detail and awe toward God. We will study this worldview's perception of God in Chapter 6.

BLUE "TruthForce" in Spiral Dynamics correlates with Maslow's "Belongingness;" Gebser "Mythic;" Fowler "Mythic/Literal Faith;" Wilber: "AMBER Absolutist."

BLUE is demonstrated in psychological human development from 7-12 years and into adulthood) We see BLUE in the young person developing causal thinking, morality, feelings of conscience and guilt, of justice and responsibility, self-control, and discipline. The young adult steps into contributing, cooperating, and conforming to the norms of their society. BLUE values show up in students who know how to work the system, employees who work hard for the system, and citizens who follow the laws.

BLUE society values monotheism, a specific social class structure with nobility or elites. It embraces authoritarian systems, nationalism, systemic racism, trade unions, law enforcement systems, bureaucracy, fundamentalism, pastor-centric churches, "born–again" Christians, and religious sects. It is the dominant worldview of Saudi Arabia, Iran, and the Indian caste system. Pyramid Structure represents BLUE, as do the Boy & Girl Scouts, Billy Graham. Law enforcement, Religious institutions, and "back to basics" educational programs.

BLUE Transcend and Include

Healthy BLUE characteristics to integrate into the next level:

- recognizes principles and order;
- concern for precise language;
- cooperates with codes of conduct;
- expects fair laws and fair penalties;
- recognition of and obsession with legal power;
- acts with caution and carefulness toward others;
- endeavors to do what's right;

- seeks foremost peace of mind;
- uses myth to teach truisms; practices neatness and cleanliness;
- BLUE functions well in industrial economies.

Unhealthy BLUE characteristics to transcend as we evolve:

- Overly dependent on authority; Resistant to risk-taking;
- Thinking only one right way;
- Fear of punishment for error;
- Resistance to the chaos of change;
- Becoming compulsive, perfectionist;
- Leads people to obey authority, and feel guilt when not conforming to group norms;
- Obsession with legal power;
- Establishment of senseless regulations;
- Over compartmentalized order;
- Emphasis on sacrificial acts; putting tradition above progress.

Unhealthy BLUE systems become repressive beasts of bureaucratic 'wait and see," inflexibility, and exclusion of anyone who breaks the rules, or questions the norms.

Life Conditions and the Transformational Dilemma

In Europe, the Roman Catholic Church was the BLUE dominant power. It managed to quash every scientific or reason-oriented endeavor and created conditions that were so stifling that the entire region under "Christendom" was suffering from poverty, illiteracy, servitude, and lack of opportunity. Nations with Authoritarian kings who couldn't respond to the people's desires were overthrown, as exemplified by the American revolution against King George and the French revolution against the bourgeois class.

BLUE's absolutism and class systems become stifling and oppressive. Reason tells us that there are gray areas, and situational ethics is more appropriate. The worldview is pushing BLUE to relax its hold and allow individuals to climb the ladder to success regardless of their family associations. The need to belong becomes less important than the need to take a chance toward self-determination, to trust reason, and to see what can be done or acquired. The BLUE worldview has been strong in the United States but has lost power in the past one hundred years or so, which is causing the obvious "Transformational Dilemma of our political and economic tension.

ORANGE vMeme: Modern, Rationalistic, Achievist

"Act in your own self-interest by playing the game to win."

**ORANGE emerged about 400 years ago, in what we call "The Enlightenment." While the BLUE consciousness was dominant, seeds of ORANGE "Modern" consciousness briefly flared throughout the world. We see glimpses of it in Greek's Golden Age of philosophy and mathematics, and again dimly during the Scholastic Period in the 1200s in Europe. ORANGE consciousness appeared in the Moslem world while Europe was in its dark ages. But the predominant BLUE Authoritarian worldview still had the power, and it managed, using authoritarian force and guilt, to keep reason at bay. ORANGE innovative rationality gained momentum during the Renaissance and emerged in a sustainable form with the Enlightenment, then the Industrial Revolution.

Modernist consciousness, equipped with an enhanced ability to reason, produced criticism of the "mythic" worldview of BLUE. "Realism," the scientific method and the accumulation of knowledge based on facts is the emphasis in the ORANGE mindset. The invention of technology (machinery, industrialization) had a pivotal impact on human consciousness. What human senses could not see and what human and animal strength could not accomplish, a machine could, and we can use them for our personal gain.

ORANGE is a self-development value system. It is driven by reason, innovation, and measurable results. It wants action and personal advancement. It values independence, and it speaks boldly against oppressive regimes such as feudalism, the Church's hierarchy, and authoritarian governments. Modernists value progress, material wealth, status, and self-improvement, and seek freedom and material gain for the sake of ease and happiness.

ORANGE is the value system that created the economic and social dynamics of the USA, with its declaration that every man is entitled to liberty, and the "pursuit of happiness." It is the prosperity of "the American Dream" shared by the millions of immigrants to the "New World." It is the first vMeme to have a global worldview, a huge step of expansion from the BLUE nationalistic worldview.

ORANGE is demonstrated in psychological human development when a person develops logical thinking and critical observation to explore one's talents and pursue a dream of self-accomplishment. Healthy ORANGE cultivates optimistic, risk-taking self-reliance.

If we look really hard, we can find a hint of ORANGE consciousness in the Wisdom writers of the Bible. We'll explore this in Chapter 7. This vMeme did not impact Christianity until after the Reformation in the 1500's CE. The most obvious form of ORANGE religion can be found in the New Thought teachings and the Law of Mind-Action. Unity, founded by Charles and Myrtle Fillmore, is identified as "Practical Christianity," which recognizes the ORANGE value of reasonable and measurable progress, within the framework of the teaching of Jesus.

Spiral Dynamics ORANGE "StriveDrive" correlates with Gebser's "Rational;" Maslow's "Self-Esteem;" Fowler's "Synthetic/ Conventional;" and Wilber's "ORANGE Multiplistic."

ORANGE Characteristics/Values:

- "I" Individualistic: "StriveDrive"
- Reason and Logic, science, and facts replace BLUE rules and herd mentality.
- Analyze and strategize to prosper
- Optimistic, risk-taking, self-reliant people "deserve their success."
- Materialistic, competitive, striving for excellence, win

- Exploratory; Entrepreneurs; personal success, "I Conceive, I Believe, I Achieve"
- Autonomy and manipulation of environment.
- Wants to win and expects everyone wants to win. Winners gain pre-eminence and perks.
- Secularism: separation of Church and State.
- Free market economy: wall street, GQ, yachts, trophy hunting. from rags to riches
- Lacks compassion. Ambitious and striving for money, status, and recognition
- Success and result-oriented and pragmatic; "You never get a second chance for a first impression."

ORANGE Transcend and Include
Healthy ORANGE characteristics to integrate:

- Values ideas and mind power; objective scientific method;
- Versatile, entrepreneurial, initiates business enterprise
- Acts on promising possibilities;
- Focused on results, progress, strategy to become better.
- Ambitious, strive for status, recognition, money.
- Sets goals and makes plans;
- Play the "game;" rags to riches
- Sees god-powers in humankind;
- Embraces cultural evolution; ha a global worldview.

Unhealthy ORANGE characteristics to transcend as we evolve:

- Acts in self-interest;
- Wants to win and assumes everyone wants to win;
- Over exploits Earth's resources for personal gain or pleasure;
- Can choose mind without heart or ethics;
- Believes solely in mind power.

We see unhealthy ORANGE in the imbalance of the economic

structure. CEOs make big salaries while their employees barely make ends meet; companies drill oil without caring for the lands and people affected by it.

The Transformational Dilemma *for Modernists is that "the pursuit of happiness" as they interpreted it doesn't offer meaningful living. When a person is exhausted with the pursuit, their soul longs for connection in relationships, with nature, with the global and local village. Additionally, people realize that not everything can be solved with reason alone. There must be a balance of reason with intuition, sensing, and feelings.*

At the societal level, ORANGE's selfish pursuits have hurt themselves, others, and the planet. "Post-Modern" GREEN offers connection and gains enough momentum to dismantle the corrupt institutions of greed and honor all beings on the planet.

GREEN: Post-Modern; Communitarian

"Seek peace within the inner self and explore, with others, the caring dimensions of community"

GREEN vMeme emerged 200 years ago. It is community oriented, a "We" or "Human-Bond" worldview. Commonly called "Post-Modern," this vMeme values egalitarianism: honoring all peoples, cultures, and creatures. GREEN's visibility in the USA emerged around the issue of slavery, and it gained momentum in the 1960s. GREEN honors diversity and empathy and wants all to be heard and understood. It can be considered the "share and care" worldview.

As a "We" value system, GREEN is often sparked into action through an emotional connection, a promise of relationship-building, or the opportunity to act to help others or save the planet. "think locally act globally, and think globally, act locally."

Characteristics/Values:

- Group-identity, "HumanBond"

- Feelings and caring supersede cold rationality. Cherish earth and life.
- Community, sensitive & humanistic. Equality & environment.
- Work motivated by human contact & contribution. Learning from others, networking.
- Being liked is more important than a competitive advantage, values openness & trust, and fears rejection & disapproval.
- Against hierarchy; judgment, and discrimination. GREEN can become "Mean GREEN" against everything and not a uniting force.
- Facilitate vs. lead. Can get too bogged down and ineffectual & revert to go-getter ORANGE.

We see a hint of GREEN consciousness in the Wisdom writers of the Bible and in Jesus' teachings, which also exhibit 2nd Tier consciousness.

GREEN "HumanBond" in Spiral Dynamics correlates with Gebser's "Pluralistic," Fowler's "Personal Reflective." Wilber: "GREEN Relativistic."

GREEN motivates improvements in race relations, environmental action, the liberation of the female population, improved elder care, and hospice care. It offers a new understanding of the body/mind relationship, healthy food, food cooperatives, and back-to-the-landers.

Indications of GREEN "Post-Modern": Society of Friends, Abolitionist movement, Underground Railroad, Women's Suffrage, the Civil Rights and Anti-Vietnam movement, unions, social outreach programs, and environmental organizations; the Progressive Left, environmental action groups, communes, cooperative housing ventures, cooperatives, the UN, and NGOs; animal rights; Habitat for Humanity, Dr's Without Borders. Democratic Socialism, Healthcare for All, Greenpeace, Politically correct, World Council of Churches. GREEN is the dominant value system in Scandinavia, the Netherlands, Canada, and California.

Transcend and Include

Healthy GREEN characteristics to integrate:

- Equality for all; Everyone should be heard;
- Cares for others and helps them;
- Self-Help, self-awareness growth
- Includes heart thinking; openly shares experiences;
- Recognizes group power; Cooperates and seeks harmony
- Dedicated to rescuing and healing the planet.
- Spiritual seeker.

Unhealthy GREEN characteristics to **transcend**:

- Susceptible to "group think," forget about each person's gift;
- Over concern about fitting in;
- Extreme caring - burnout;
- Insistence on collective problem-solving;
- Focus on resisting rather than finding solutions;
- Intolerant of other's worldviews;
- Influenced by others' opinions;
- Overwhelmed by group power.

GREEN can be arrogant, elitist, and judgmental, sensing its superiority over the other worldviews, insisting that its worldview is the only right way. Don Beck called it "the mean green meme," explaining that it can display "strong egocentric narcissism combined with pontification about humanity and equality."[76]

The Transformational Dilemma of Post-Modernism is that "caring and sharing" is naïvely insufficient for the complexity of the global community. GREEN's idealism is blind: Don Beck observes that 9/11/2001 "was a wakeup call, and for the first time GREEN began to see the ugly face of RED/BLUE." GREEN aims at peaceful co-existence but is often driven by fear and anger. GREEN's insistence on consensus decision-making does not lend itself to expedient solutions. With the complexity presented to the world today, we seek a more expedited way to adjust, flow, and make decisions.

2nd Tier: Integral: "A MOMENTOUS LEAP"

> *Humans must prepare for a momentous leap…The present moment finds our society attempting to negotiate the most difficult, but at the same time the most exciting transition humans have faced to date. It is not merely a transition to a new level of existence but the start of a new 'movement' in the symphony of human history."* –Clare Graves[77]

2nd Tier marks a quantum consciousness shift.

Tier One is characterized as a "having and doing" mindset, driven by ego survival. The 2nd Tier is a "being" mindset, driven by a desire to be authentic. The life-changing shift into YELLOW is a giant leap because it's the most challenging (to the ego). The fears of the previous stages, all attached to survival, are replaced with caution and curiosity about just being alive in the expansive universe.

2nd Tier can take in multiple perspectives. After moving through the stages of the 1st Tier, where we can perceive the world only through our own worldview, in the 2nd Tier we can understand and empathize with the worldviews we have journeyed through and can aptly assist others who are moving a value shift. The 2nd Tier of the Spiral is aptly called "integral," because it has done the work of "*transcend and include*," integrating and valuing what came before. Unique talents and dispositions are honored as contributing something valuable to the whole. Although 2nd Tier consciousness is not perfection or complete enlightenment, it is a level that is not driven by ego.

YELLOW: Integrative, Systemic

"Live fully and responsibility as what you are and what you learn to become."

YELLOW VMeme: 50 years ago. "I"

In keeping with the predictable pattern of the Spiral, this is a shift into individual expression. YELLOW drops group-think fear and assumptions. YELLOW is critical and curious but practices

173

non-judgment. YELLOW is creative, innovative, and likes challenges. It has a thirst to learn for its own sake and keeps asking questions and seeking solutions. It is oriented toward Systems Thinking: how parts interact to create the greater whole and it is comfortable with a flex-flow approach, comfortable with chaos and change.

YELLOW's thought searches for the quality and depth of thinking/feeling that can deal with complex problems. Its mindset is agile, able to have a "flex/flow" response to life conditions. It focuses on functionality, disposing of norms that are no longer useful. It acknowledges and practices personal responsibility.

YELLOW has just emerged and is manifesting as people begin to imagine integrative structures to solve problems produced by previous structures. Its focus on systems thinking and "Third-Way" politics is offering answers to systemic issues such as racism in policing and corrections. Having consciously integrated the previous subsistence stages, YELLOW is capable of reflecting upon each to examine what healthy values we should include, and which unhealthy behaviors must be released.

In personal human development, the YELLOW worldview practices acceptance of every aspect of self. For example, the contemplation of the PURPLE level may lead a person into an artistic form of expression to enliven the magical, spiritual intuition that was pushed aside at an earlier time. An Integral practitioner might recognize their inherent RED values and needs, then consciously participate in a competition of some kind, while keeping the ego in control. Or one might use RED characteristics when standing up for oneself or expressing one's boundaries. The contemplation of the BLUE level allows the integral thinker to empathize with a fundamentalist friend's ideas, while dis-identifying with their worldview, or to seek a position on the school board or planning commission. While honoring their Modern world, they release the need to manipulate their environment and focus on their responsibility toward the world, without hurling the emotional accusations of the Post-Modern.

YELLOW "FlexFlow" in Spiral Dynamics correlates with Maslow's Self-Actualization;" Fowler "Universalizing Faith;" Wilber: "TEAL Integral."

YELLOW is emerging in conjunction with TURQUOISE

TURQUOISE: Holistic, Global, Synergy

"Experience the whole of existence through mind and spirit."

TURQUOISE vMeme emerged approximately 50 years ago. It has a "we" orientation. This holistic worldview can honor many perspectives and can also see one global community, an elegantly balanced system of interdependent forces. Its focus is to experience the wholeness of existence through body, mind, and spirit. It is manifesting as intuitive awareness of the unity of the entire system. TURQUOISE engages collective human intelligence without sacrificing individuality.

The concept of the interconnection of all belongs to the TURQUOISE worldview. (extended-mind, morphic fields, non-locality, collective unconscious, Noosphere, Akashic Records.) Rather than thinking of these ideas in religious terms, TURQUOISE values scientific research and data tested objectively by standard scientific methodology to confirm such ideas. Remarkable data confirms communication between this field of consciousness and individual minds.

TURQUOISE is aware of an underlying reality that has for millennia supported intuitive mythological spirituality. It finds new methods to realize its usable energy and power. We are beginning to discover that higher consciousness can use leverage as effective in solving problems of life conditions as the computer is in solving an immense number of problems.

TURQUOISE "GlobalView" in Spiral Dynamics correlates with Wilber: "TEAL Integral."

Perception of God Through the TURQUOISE Lens

In the TURQUOISE vMeme the perception of the nature of the Divine changes; not what or who to worship, but the recognition of a ceaseless, restless creative energy in the Universe; harmonizing energy supporting the individual and the collective in the manifesting of God Self.

> *"Someday, after mastering the winds, the waves, the tides and gravity, we shall harness for God the energies of love, and then, for a second time in the history of the world, man will have discovered fire."* - Teilhard de Chardin

Healthy Characteristics of 2nd Tier

- Feels a connection with all humans.
- Uses this connection for support.
- Studies the field of consciousness.
- Seeks to know everything.
- Both collectivist and individualist
- Perceives extended time/place.
- Seeks longevity and productivity.

Like the 1st Tier, there are 6 levels identified in the 2nd Tier: YELLOW, TURQUOISE, CORAL, TEAL, AUBERGINE...

Processing This Information:

1. Check your knowledge: Give a short statement of your understanding of each of the 1st Tier v Memes' codes and values and assumptions about the world. (BEIGE, PURPLE, RED, BLUE, ORANGE, GREEN)
2. Consider your personal emotional, social, and spiritual development considering the Spiral. Do you see yourself moving through each of these worldviews as you grew up? Do you feel that you might have sort of skipped one? How might you make sense of this? How might you encourage yourself to revisit that value system and reconcile with it?

3. Notice what insights or questions you gained regarding the evolution of collective consciousness from this introduction to Spiral Dynamics. (such as culture, history, politics, and economics. etc.)

4. Consider Robert Brumet's words from his book *Birthing a Greater Reality*: "personal transformation and global evolution are inseparable." … "we have innately connected in a broader web." "the ultimate potential of human consciousness: to consciously merge its identity with the Absolute or "God." …

5. We witnessed and experienced the effects of a major shift in worldviews as I wrote this book in 2019-2022. One major life condition that has catapulted us into this shift is the worldwide COVID-19 pandemic. Other systemic problems like race relations and income inequality are coming out of the shadows. One flash-point was the heartless public murder of George Floyd, an innocent man, by law enforcers, inciting mobs of masked voices of protest. Another was the attack on the people's house the US Capital on January 6, 2021. It is a momentous time worldwide. The Transformational Dilemma is palpable. All the levels are affected by these life conditions and all levels are responding according to their worldview. Consider how each level is voicing their pain. Examples: civilian violence, volunteer militia groups, looters (RED); Police Violence with the peaceful protesters (BLUE protecting the ORANGE system.) Black Lives Matter protesters: (GREEN); the sudden interest in learning how to be an anti-racist. (exit-GREEN, exiting out of angry GREEN into a more mature "Post-Post Modern") As GREEN reconsiders the institutions of racism, economics, and healthcare, it wants to make laws that enforce *community, opportunity, responsibility, and accountability.* ORANGE is fighting to keep its economic stronghold, even as it knows that the materialistic worldview isn't meeting the needs of the whole. BLUE and RED are struggling to preserve their traditions and customs in a world where ORANGE and

GREEN have taken over. Simultaneously, Emerging Yellow invites exiting GREEN to engage in creating consciously from an integral worldview, considering the values and needs of each previous worldview. GREEN answers ORANGE's discontent, declaring that this rising desire to connect with others is valued over material gain. The Spiral teaches us not to "throw the baby out with the bathwater." Healthy GREEN and emerging YELLOW remember that we want to "include" the Healthy ORANGE (reason, science, setting goals, and acting on them.)

About the Author

Rev Pat Veenema, M.Div. grew up in the baby boomer generation in a huge "tribe" of 50-some grandchildren of Dutch emigrants. Her maternal great grandfather was a Christian educator from The Netherlands, who came to America to help develop educational programs in what would become Eastern Christian School Association of Northern New Jersey. Her childhood worldview rose out of this close-knit Dutch-American Calvinist community, where education about the Bible, considered the inspired, infallible, exclusive revelation of God, was a daily essential part of her K–12 education. In high school, Pat organized and led peer group Bible Studies before the tardy bell. She earned her BA and a teaching certificate from Calvin University, ("Calvin College" in the '70s) Grand Rapids MI, where Calvin's Institutes were studied as part of the core curriculum, and where, to her dismay, attending seminary was *verboten* to women.

After graduation, Pat and her husband conscientiously removed themselves from the Dutch American tribe and invested their twenties and thirties serving communities in the Appalachian mountains of southern Virginia and Kentucky, teaching public school pre-teens from coal and tobacco families, and building "warm-and-dry" houses. They engaged in social activism and spiritual explorations with many Interfaith peace-lovers: the Society of Friends, Catholics, Methodists, Presbyterians, UCC, Unitarians. They raised their two daughters in a progressive neighborhood in Durham, NC, working with Witness For Peace and teaching in public schools filled with precious and precocious children of all colors, many who came to school hungry every morning.

Typical of the GREEN activist, Pat "crashed" at mid-life, thus beginning a steady and determined recovery through mental and spiritual metamorphosis. After years of peeling away the layers, Pat had come to see and accept her divine nature and was ready to respond to the intuitive call to ministry that she had sensed at age 20. She earned her long-envisioned master's degree, attending Unity Institute and Seminary in Lee's Summit Missouri. While serving her first church appointment, she realized that her passion to teach was still very strong. She founded New Vista Learning Center and has maintained a flourishing online spiritual school since 2015, supporting and inspiring the next generation of Unity students who are just curious or on their own path to ministry. She subsequently became adjunct faculty at her Alma Mater (aka Unity Worldwide Spiritual Institute) where she is highly regarded as a teacher who knows how to make an online learning experience a joy.

Endnotes

1   Fillmore, Charles *Mysteries of Genesis*, (Unity Village, MO, Unity Books, 1936), p. 171

2   Fillmore, Charles: from a lecture delivered in 1897. *Talks on Truth* (Unity Village, MO, Unity Books, 1926), p. 17

Chapter 1

3   H. Emilie Cady, "Unity of the Spirit," *Lessons in Truth: A Course of Twelve Lessons in Practical Christianity* Centennial Edition (Kansas City: Unity School of Christianity, 1919), 157-158.

4   Pew Foundation Survey 2018, https://www.pewforum.org/2018/04/25/when-americans-say-they-believe-in-god-what-do-they-mean/ (accessed February 24, 2020).

5   Marcus J. Borg *Reading the Bible Again for the First Time: Taking the Bible Seriously but Not Literally*. Harper San Francisco 2001. Page 4

6   https://americanhumanist.org/what-is-humanism/reasons-humanists-reject-bible/

7   "Modern" and "Post-Modern" are capitalized because they refer to specific stages in the evolutionary model applied to this study.

8   Israel Finkelstein and Neil Asher Silberman, *The Bible Unearthed: Archaeology's New Vision of Ancient Israel and The origin of its Sacred Texts*. (Touchstone, New York, 2001), 61.

9   Crash Course in Torah: Session 3: *Patriarchs and Matriarchs of the Jewish People*. Avraham Goldhar 4:04 minutes. https://youtu.be/stMsjlztCxY

10 As mentioned, the Bible has influenced literature. This phrase became the title of a popular book by Lois Lowry about a family of Jews during WWII.

11 No, this is not a typo! The water they crossed is actually called the "Sea of Reeds" or the "Reed Sea." The Sea of Reeds (or seaweed) was a shallow body of water in the Nile delta that doesn't exist today. Red Sea is a very wide body of water between Africa and Asia.

12 Grant L. Voth, "The History of World Literature," Great Courses Plus. Produced by The Teaching Company, 2007.

Chapter 2

13 Don Edward Beck and Christopher C. Cowan, *Spiral Dynamics: Mastering Values, Leadership and Change* (Oxford, UK: Blackwell Publishing, Ltd., 1996). 41, 45.
14 Beck and Cowan, *Spiral Dynamics: Mastering Values, Leadership and Change*. 41, 46.
15 Beck and Cowan, *Spiral Dynamics: Mastering Values, Leadership and Change*. 41, 46.
16 Beck and Cowan, *Spiral Dynamics: Mastering Values, Leadership and Change*. 41.

Chapter 3

17 Friedman, Richard Elliott. *Who Wrote the Bible* (New York, Harper & Row 1987), 19.
18 Translation by Richard Elliott Friedman, *The Bible With Sources Revealed: A New View into the Five Books of Moses* (New York, Harper Collins. 2003), 35.
19 Friedman, *Who Wrote the Bible,* 265 footnote.
20 Ibid., 65.
21 Translation by Richard Elliott Friedman from *The Bible with Sources Revealed,* 93–94.
22 Friedman, *The Bible with Sources Revealed,* 153 footnote.
23 Don Edward Beck and Christopher C. Cowan, *Spiral Dynamics: Mastering Values, Leadership and Change* (Oxford, UK: Blackwell Publishing, Ltd., 1996). 41.

Chapter 4

24 Translation of Genesis 28:17-18 by Richard Elliot Friedman, *The Bible With Sources Revealed: A New View into the Five Books of Moses* (New York: HarperCollins, 2003), 65. I chose Friedman's wording of "the gate of the skies," which more accurately depicts the common cosmology of the time.
25 Translation of Genesis 33:20 by Friedman, 87. I used this translation to illustrate that the E writer used "El" to refer to God. E does not use the name YHWH until it is revealed as such to Moses in Exodus 4. (same book, page 4)
26 Translation of Numbers 22:31 by Friedman, *The Bible With Sources Revealed*
27 "Immanent" in theological terms means omnipresent, knowable, perceivable, active in the world.
28 Translation of Genesis 22:19 by Richard Elliot Friedman, *The Bible With Sources Revealed*

29   Richard Elliot Friedman, *The Bible With Sources Revealed*. This comes from one of Friedman's' fantastic footnotes. 65.

30   Ken Wilber *Up from Eden* Quest Books, Wheaton, IL 1981.

Chapter 5

31   Beck and Cowan. *Spiral Dynamics*. 41

32   Israel Finkelstein and Neil Asher Silberman, *The Bible Unearthed: Archaeology's New Vision of Ancient Israel and The origin of its Sacred Texts*. (Touchstone, New York, 2001), 60.

33   Finkelstein and Silberman, *The Bible Unearthed*, 88-89.

34   The J writer authored most of Judges 8-21, with the exception of a few phrases inserted at the beginning and end of chapters. Richard Elliott Friedman, *The Hidden Book in the Bible*

Chapter 6

35   Karen Armstrong, *The Great Transformation: The Beginning of Our Religious Traditions* (New York: Anchor Books, 2007), 42-56.

36   Finkelstein and Silberman, *The Bible Unearthed*, 24.

37   Don Edward Beck and Christopher C. Cowan, *Spiral Dynamics: Mastering Values, Leadership and Change* (Oxford, UK: Blackwell Publishing, Ltd., 1996). 41

38   Adela Oppenheim, Curator, Department of Egyptian Art, "Sunday at The Met—Ancient Egypt Transformed: The Middle Kingdom" (The Met Lecture, New York, NY, October 25, 2015). https://www.metmuseum.org/metmedia/video/lectures/sam-ancient-egypt-transformed (Accessed 12/11/2021) minute 11: 04

39   Richard Elliot Friedman, *The Exodus* (New York, HarperCollins, 2017), 203-204.

40   Paul R. Smith, *Integral Christianity* (St. Paul, MN, Paragon House 2011), 80.

41   *Or I AM WHAT I AM,* or *I WILL BE WHAT I WILL BE.* (footnote in NRSV translation*)*

42   Spiral Dynamics uses upper and lower case deliberately. It is a way of indicating more specifically where someone is in the spectrum of the stage. ALL CAPS indicates the predominant consciousness. Lower case indicates that this vMeme is less influential but is still an active dynamic in the person's worldview. For example, purple/RED indicates that the writer is predominantly coming from the RED worldview but has significant PURPLE thoughts, values and norms. If written in reverse, for example RED/blue, the person is operating predominantly from the RED perspective, and is stretching into the next paradigm.

43 Translation of Exodus 35:10 by Richard Elliott Friedman, *The Bible With Sources Revealed: A New View into the Five Books of Moses* New York, Harper Collins. 2003, 178.

44 Richard Elliot Friedman, *The Hidden Book in the Bible* (New York NY, HarperCollins 1998). Friedman does not list the verses per se. He translated J's writings, identifying them with the same format as in the Bible. All of J's writings are on pages with a black margin.

45 Israel Finkelstein and Neil Asher Silberman, *The Bible Unearthed. Pages 48-71.*

46 Life Conditions is a Spiral Dynamics term. See Appendix

47 Armstrong, *The Great Transformation,* 48.

Chapter 7

48 Karen Armstrong *The Great Transformation: The Beginning of Our Religious Traditions),* xvii. Karl Jaspers dubbed the eighth to third centuries BCE "The Axial Age."

49 Richard Elliott Friedman, *Who Wrote the Bible* (New York, Harper & Row 1987), 213

50 Richard Elliott Friedman, *Who Wrote the Bible* 152.

51 Translation by Richard Elliott Friedman, *The Bible with Sources Revealed* (New York, NY, HarperCollins, 2003), 356.

52 Don Edward Beck and Christopher C. Cowan, *Spiral Dynamics: Mastering Values, Leadership and Change* (Oxford, UK: Blackwell Publishing, Ltd., 1996). 41

53 Shema Judaism. Encyclopaedia Britannica https://www.britannica.com/topic/Shema (Accessed 12/15/21)

54 1 and 2 Chronicles, Ezra, and Nehemiah were traditionally considered Wisdom Writings. These three books might have been written by the same author, after 400 BCE, yet some parts appear to be written as late as 200 BCE. 1 and 2 Chronicles were originally one book, as were Ezra and Nehemiah. Chronicles re-tells the history of the Jewish people, from Adam to the Babylonian exile. Ezra-Nehemiah picks up the story of the Israelites at the end of the exile and records their re-establishment of Judah. The writers painstakingly recorded every legitimate specific family name, location, and ancestral house associated with the Jewish people and reported on the priests dedication to purifying the land of all non-Jews. Speaking from an evolutionary viewpoint, these books serve to reinforce the authoritarian nature and exclusivism of Judaism, which was exactly their intention.

55 Karen Armstrong, *The Great Transformation,* 438.

56 The Greek translation of the Hebrew bible is called the "Septuagint."

57 "Non-canonical" refers to the books that are not included in the Protestant Bible but are included in the Bibles of the Roman Catholic and the Greek Orthodox Churches. In the case of First and Second Maccabees, they are not included in the Hebrew Bible nor the Protestant Bible because they have a doubtful origin (apocryphal).

58 Curd, Patricia, "Presocratic Philosophy", *The Stanford Encyclopedia of Philosophy* (Fall 2020), Edward N. Zalta (ed.), https://plato.stanford.edu/archives/fall2020/entries/presocratics/

Chapter 8

59 H. Emilie Cady, "Unity of the Spirit," *Lessons in Truth: A Course of Twelve Lessons in Practical Christianity* Centennial Edition (Kansas City: Unity School of Christianity, 1919), 162.

60 See *The 8 Points of Progressive Christianity* https://progressivechristianity.org/the-8-points/

61 Marcus Borg, *Reading the Bible Again for the First Time* (HarperCollins, New York, NY, 2001), 123-127.

62 Paraphrase of John 20:15 While EJ Niles taught this course at Unity Institute, she would often ask if we were feeling like Mary in the garden when she asked this of the "gardener."

63 H. Emilie Cady, "Unity of the Spirit," *Lessons in Truth: A Course of Twelve Lessons in Practical Christianity* (Kansas City: Unity School of Christianity, 1919).

64 Steve McIntosh, *Integral Consciousness, and the Future of Evolution: How the Integral Worldview Is Transforming Politics, Culture and Spirituality* (St Paul, MN: Paragon House, 2007), 124.

65 Dustin DiPerna, "Wake up, Grow up, Clean up, Show up, Excerpt from The Coming Waves" *Integral World: Exploring Theories of Everything* (October 2014) https://www.integralworld.net/diperna06.html

66 Edwin Holwerda *Spiral Dynamics: Beautiful Noise (Dr. Don Beck)*, March 22,2014. https://youtu.be/WvlJ66kUcfg (Accessed Jan. 2022)

67 Jessica Roemischer, "The Never-Ending Upward Quest: An interview with Dr. Don Beck" *What is Enlightenment: Redefining Spirituality for an Evolving World*, Issue 22 (Fall-Winter 2002): 17. https://www.integralheartfoundation.org/spiraldynamics.pdf (Accessed Nov 26 2021), 22.

Appendix

68 Fillmore, Charles *Mysteries of Genesis*, published 1936, (Kansas City: Unity House 1903).page 171

69 Fillmore, Charles *Talks on Truth* a lecture from 1897 page 17

70 Theodore Andrea Cook, *The Curves of Life* (1914)

71 Dawkins, Richard *The Selfish Gene* (1976)

72 https://www.goodreads.com/author/quotes/5387.Pierre_Teilhard_de_Chardin

73 Wilber, Ken. *Up from Eden*, 1981

74 Bela H. Banathy. *Guided Evolution of Society* page 107

75 www./spiraldynamicsintegral.nl/en/red/

76 "What Is Enlightenment" magazine Issue 22 Fall Winter 2002 p. 17 spiraldynamics_WhatIsEnlightenment.pdf

77 "What Is Enlightenment" magazine Issue 22 Fall Winter 2002 p.23 spiraldynamics_WhatIsEnlightenment.pdf

Printed in the United States
by Baker & Taylor Publisher Services